The Old-Time Brand-Name Cookbook

The Old-Time Brand-Name Cookbook

Recipes, Illustrations, and Advice
from the Early Kitchens of America's
Most Trusted Food Makers

BUNNY CRUMPACKER

ABRADALE PRESS
HARRY N. ABRAMS, INC., PUBLISHERS

Editorial Director: Elizabeth Viscott Sullivan
Editor: Tricia Levi
Designer: Kay Schuckhart/Blond on Pond

Library of Congress Catalog Card Number: 97–62144
ISBN 0–8109–8209–9

Printed in Hong Kong

Abradale Press
Harry N. Abrams, Inc.
100 Fifth Avenue
New York, N.Y. 10011
www.abramsbooks.com

For Chick

e   n   t   s

*T*oday's simplest kitchen operation—breakfast, maybe, or tea and cookies in the afternoon—meant hours of work a century ago, usually by several people. There were no gas or electric stoves, no refrigerators, no canned foods, no packaged foods. Forget microwaves and supermarkets—that would have been science fiction, which also didn't exist yet.

Yesterday's Kitchen: The Early Days of Convenience Cooking

Keeping a kitchen and feeding a family was day-long work. It meant labor that had to begin long before anybody's stomach produced an empty rumble.

About the middle of the nineteenth century, the open hearth was gradually replaced by the iron stove. It burned either wood or coal—hours of work in either case. Coal had to be shoveled, and wood had to be cut and stacked; cold ashes had to be scooped out and disposed of; the fire had to be laid and started; once going, it had to be stoked and replenished; the oven temperature had to be guessed at and then maintained. When the cooking was done, the stove had to be polished to keep it presentable. And then the ashes had to be scooped out again.

In the morning, the chickens had to be fed and the eggs gathered. The cow had to be milked. The butter had to be churned from yesterday's milk. The pig had already been slaughtered and the side smoked; now the bacon had to be sliced. Only when all this had been done could the cook put on her apron and actually begin to cook.

In order to keep all this going three times a day, along with cleaning, washing, ironing, sewing, mending, and child care, most houses, even those at the lowest income levels, depended upon servants. Nearly everybody had at least one girl in the kitchen; in the South, she was usually Black, in the North and the West, a recent immigrant. Families with more money employed a maid as well as a cook. In the grandest households, there were simply dozens of servants. The ratio of waiters to guests at a formal dinner

What a comfort to have an abundant supply of luxurious hot water—all you want—at any time, for dish-washing, for bathing, and for all housekeeping needs. It can be yours with an Automatic Storage Gas Water Heater.

"The Associated Customer,"
Associated Gas and Electric, 1929

in the 1850s was supposed to be one to four, which is why there was also a butler who supervised the staff.

The single girl in the kitchen had basically the same chores as the staff in the big house on the hill. Duties were not determined by finances; dinner depended on what was available. There were no refrigerators—instead there were cold cellars and, later, ice boxes. Cookbooks offered recipes for sour milk baking as well as for fresh. There was no baking powder, no powdered gelatin, no ground coffee. White sugar was scarce, expensive, and cumbersome (it was sold in chunks, sometimes in huge cones, covered with net to keep flies away, and then hung from the ceiling to be chipped at when needed).

Canned foods, except for preserves, were new and considered potentially dangerous. Fresh vegetables and fruits were available in the summer and fall, but by winter and spring, all that was left were cabbage and potatoes and those root vegetables that could make it through the winter, kept in a cold cellar or the near-frozen soil. Pickles added bursts of flavor to a bland diet.

Farmers' wives (in the first half of the nineteenth century, 90% of the American population lived on farms) raised their own food and traded (the derivation of butter and egg money) for the few things they couldn't provide for themselves: sugar, salt, pepper, tea, coffee, flour, and such treats as raisins and chocolate. Some farmers grew their own sorghum cane, and their wives pressed it, and boiled the juice down to make molasses. In towns and cities, housewives depended on peddlers and market stalls, and the peddlers and marketers depended in turn upon erratic shipments, by boat or wagon, of meat and staples. No one ran out to the corner store for a quart of milk; instead, the milk pail was carried to the cow. In the poorer parts of cities, families bought "swill milk," from scrawny cows that had been fed on distillery wastes. Swill milk was yellowish, and sometimes the cow's owner would whiten it with chalk.

The Kitchen Revolution Begins

It was the Industrial Revolution that caused the Kitchen Revolution. There were new inventions, and then, suddenly, there were factories to manufacture them. Factory work demanded little skill and paid better than kitchen work. Certainly the hours were better. Household help became more and more scarce. But household help became less and less necessary, because of the factories. It was a paradox and a circle: The factories took the labor force away from the kitchens and the parlors, but gave back the products that replaced the labor.

By the 1840s, the new iron stove was becoming the center of kitchen work, as the hearth had been before it. It was compact, off the floor, and relatively efficient. It burned wood or coal. But the true beginning of the new era was marked by the arrival of the first gas stove in the 1850s. It was patented in 1866 but for a long time, people were afraid of it. It was to be thirty years more—a generation—before the gas stove appeared less sinister. How very devilishly easy it must have seemed, a sulfuric sort of marvel, simply to turn a handle and have a flame appear. No wonder no one trusted it! In Puritan America, where work was virtue, the gas stove seemed a product of Lucifer himself. Indeed, it did occasionally blow up.

The first electric range was exhibited in London in 1891. By 1913, it had begun to appear on the market. On the cold front, things were moving at the same pace. The cold cellar and the ice house were supplemented in about 1830 by the ice box with its huge chunk of melting ice and its drip pan, which had to be emptied every day. Some families, the more fastidious, maybe, or perhaps just those with nervous husbands, kept their ice boxes on the back porch so that the ice man wouldn't have to trek through the house. Mama had to go outside, though, fairly often.

By the early 1900s, gas refrigerators had followed the trail blazed by gas stoves into modern kitchens. The first electric refrigerator, with its important looking round top—machined art deco—was sold in 1916. It cost about $900, a truly staggering sum then—more than a new car. Two decades later, the electric refrigerator, with its tiny freezer section for "cubed ice," was affordable and indispensible.

As the population of America increased and the horizon moved west, placing farms farther from consumers, the demand for more and better preserved food accelerated, and the means followed.

The First Processed Foods

In France, Louis Pasteur learned to sterilize milk and to inoculate sheep and hogs against anthrax. In America, Gail Borden, the son of a frontiersman who became the first of many food innovators, invented a dehydrated meat biscuit. Sure it

YOU CAN PREPARE
MEALS IN ADVANCE...

With your General Electric Refrigerator to aid you, you can do much of your meal preparation in advance by putting to good use those "odd moments" which occur in every household every day.... Here are some of the things you can do which will relieve that last-minute confusion at mealtime and leave you free to enjoy the company of your family and guests:

- *Make up salad dressings, put into jars.*
- *Prepare lettuce or other salad greens.*
- *Mix up a recipe for Refrigerator Rolls.*
- *Make a supply of pastry, wrap in waxed paper.*
- *Make aspic jelly and keep in jars.*
- *Make a batch of Refrigerator Cookie dough, wrap in waxed paper.*

- *Make medium thick white sauce and keep in tightly covered jar. It will be ready for creamed soups, vegetables, or for escalloped dishes.*
- *Look over the dinner menu and see what can be done in advance.*

Often as many as three meals can be prepared at one time.

"Silent Hostess Treasure Book,"
GE Refrigerators, 1930

Borden's

Evaporated
Milk
Book of Recipes

meant his fortune, he spent all his own money and everything he could borrow to fund a trip to London to the International Exposition of 1852. Things didn't go well, and he had to come back by steerage (perhaps eating his own biscuits). On the ship, he saw hundreds of families crowded together. He watched immigrant children, huddled in miserable spaces with their families, grow sick and die from drinking the milk of infected cows, kept on board to furnish milk, cream, and butter. Once back home, he did not forget what he had seen. Four years later, he patented a process for condensing and canning milk. This was the birth of the age of convenience food. It was no longer necessary to be personally acquainted with a cow in order to have a reliable source of milk.

No one then could have foreseen what the logical extension of Gail Borden's evaporated milk would be: hamburger extender and frozen biscuits, dehydrated marshmallows and imitation blueberries. The road to instant rice and cake mix was marked by the invention of products we no longer think of as "processed" or "convenience." It's almost as if they grew that way, perhaps in the peanut butter fields or hanging from the instant coffee trees.

From our perspective, it seems as if all these changes took place in a parade, each product going proudly by, in a series of small and inevitable steps forward.

In 1890, Charles B. Knox watched his wife making calves' foot jelly. It was a tedious process requiring hours of simmering in order for the broth to reduce enough to gel after it cooled. Perhaps Mr. Knox missed his wife's company; perhaps he minded the smell; perhaps he thought Mrs. Knox spent too much time in the kitchen; perhaps he knew a good idea when he had one.

He was a salesman. He had heard of powdered gelatin. It occurred to him to package powdered gelatin in small quantities for easy use in the home kitchen. Mrs. Knox worked out a collection of recipes to be given away with

> *You have no doubt noticed, while pouring the hot water on some gelatines, a sickening odor which will arise from it (this never will happen in pure gelatines), and shows that the stock is not pure, so is unfit for food.*

Knox Gelatin, c. 1895

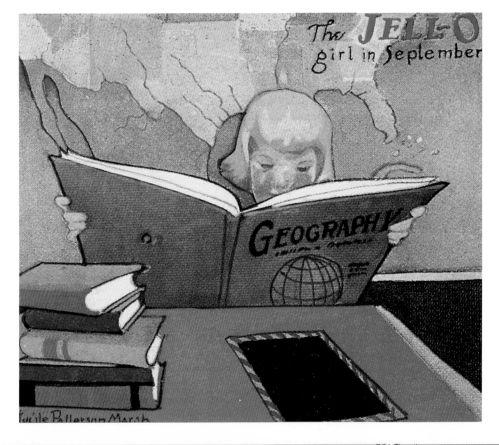

their gelatin, to show how easily it could be used with consistent and fine results. The union of taste and convenience—love and marriage—was on its way into millions of kitchens.

Jell-O came along a few years later, the next logical step. A couple in upstate New York thought of adding sugar and fruit flavoring to the gelatin. All that was needed was to convince housewives that the sweet powder in the little square box would change their lives. Recipe booklets were issued, giving dozens of ways to ring the changes

The JELL-O girl in September

GEOGRAPHY

Lucile Patterson Marsh

The JELL-O
girl in December

on Jell-O. There were recipes for desserts and salads that could be made in minutes, that would always taste the same, and that were guaranteed to be fail-safe. Jell-O, and jelled food in general, became status food: You had to be able to keep it cold. That meant you had an ice box, and that was, for a while at least, a mark of status. It sometimes seemed as if anything that could be eaten could be jelled—from the first course to the last, from soup to nuts. The Jell-O pamphlets, published by the company that bought the recipe for the sweetened powder, include recipes for soups, salads, and meat as well as endless varieties of dessert puddings. Jell-O was bought by the

Genesee Pure Food Company, and then was itself purchased by the Postum Company in that company's expansion move in the mid-1920s; Postum eventually became General Foods.

The beverage Postum was part of the process that resulted in the hundreds of varieties of breakfast cereal we are presented with today. But breakfast cereal owes something to indigestion, too.

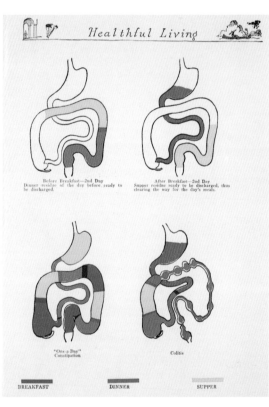

Digestive problems were rampant a hundred years ago, for many reasons: lack of refrigeration, for one; hygiene problems, for another; a heavy, greasy diet with insufficient fiber, for a third. Patent medicines were hawked from coast to coast, but they were not preventative, and frequently not really curative, either. One of the first to address the causes of all the intestinal aches and pains of the age was the Reverend Sylvester Graham—who gave us Graham crackers and Graham flour. He believed that flour caused all the trouble, and he promoted whole-grain unsifted flour as a cure-all. He was also a teetotaler and a vegetarian, and opposed to spices on the ground that they were aphrodisiacs. One of his disciples founded the Western Health Reform Institute in 1866, and a few years after that, Dr. John Harvey Kellogg was hired as manager and changed the name of the Institute to the Battle Creek Sanitarium.

Among the procedures at the Sanitarium: Patients who were underweight were fed twenty-six times a day, and between meals had to lie motionless in bed with sandbags on their stomachs on the theory that this would help their bodies

D Y S P E P S I A   O U R   N A T I O N A L   D I S E A S E

Wherever men and women are allured by the fascinations of business life and social endeavor away from the simple and natural life it is not an exaggeration to say that nine out of ten of them are either sufferers from chronic indigestion or from occasional derangements of the stomach or bowels.

Many sociologists declare, indeed, that most of our crimes may be traced to indigestion.

"Shredded Wheat Dishes," Shredded Wheat, 1910

absorb the nutrients they needed. Physical activity of any kind was forbidden to them—they were not even allowed to brush their teeth—because moving would burn up the calories they needed so badly. Patients with high blood pressure ate grapes. Just grapes. Between ten and fourteen pounds a day. Enormous attention was given to what went into bodies, and what came out of them.

Dr. Kellogg had been influenced by another nineteenth century food faddist, Horace Fletcher, who believed that much of the digestive process took place in the mouth; therefore food should stay in the mouth as long as possible. The way

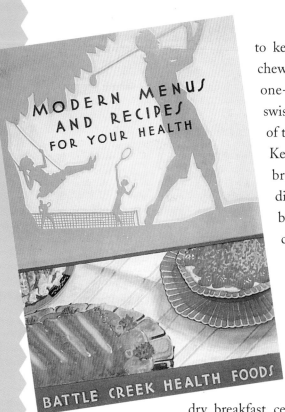

to keep it there was to chew, and chew, and chew: every mouthful had to be chewed at least one-hundred times. (Liquids were to be swished around in the mouth for a minimum of thirty seconds before they were swallowed.) Kellogg gave his guests hard crackers at breakfast, and chewing them proved difficult—digestive problems were on the brink of being replaced by dental ones. Dry cereal—corn flakes—made life easier.

One of the patients at the San, as the Battle Creek Sanatorium was fondly known, was Charles W. Post. He had an ulcer, and was forbidden to drink tea or coffee. He developed a beverage made from grains, and eponymously called it Postum. He also came up with his own dry breakfast cereals, Grape-Nuts and Post Toasties. A Grape-Nuts pamphlet published by the Postum Company assures us that the "nut-like granules" offer "just enough resistance to the teeth."

And so the kitchen revolution continued, with factory-made product after product making life in the kitchen easier. In 1894, a sailor at a boardinghouse in Boston complained because the puddings served up at dinner were too lumpy. He had seen tapioca pounded in mortars in the South Seas so it would be easier to use, and he suggested that the cook grind her tapioca before cooking. The result: lump-free puddings. She began to sell ground tapioca to her neighbors. Business boomed; she called her new product "Minute Tapioca." It was the first minute food to be so designated. It added the awareness of the virtue of speed to the housewife's burgeoning convenience consciousness.

Preserving food had always been an important part of kitchen work, carrying the home through the winter, through the lean times. Salting, curing, smoking, sugaring—all of these came ages before canning and freezing. And so did pickling, in brine and in vinegar, in crocks and in barrels. Mason jars appeared in the mid-nineteenth century, and cans came later. They'd been around, but they weren't really safe. In the late 1870s, a new method of canning under steam pressure was developed; it meant reducing heating time, it was safer, and it made possible the commercial production of canned goods. It meant the housewife could now buy the pickles she'd always had to put up herself.

Henry J. Heinz began by selling pickles to groceries around Sharpsburg, Pennsylvania in 1869. His "57 Varieties" were synonymous with pickles and ketchup for years. In 1893, his display at the Chicago World's Fair was a smash hit. More than one-million people visited, tasting samples, and taking home tiny green metal Heinz pickles to add to their key chains or charm bracelets. In New York City, a six-story green pickle bearing the letters H-E-I-N-Z stood where Fifth Avenue crossed Twenty-third Street, until the Flatiron Building took the pickle's place.

In 1898, John T. Torrance, who had a Ph.D. in chemistry, figured out how to solve the problem of the large cans the manufacturers of soup needed for their products. Condensed soup was the answer, and the Joseph P. Campbell Company of Camden, New Jersey was the result, another entry on the time-line of processed food production.

What a difference there is between the active life of a savage and our modern living conditions. We live in a tempo of tensions. Our nerves are taut. Our minds are working under pressure all the time. We sit at a desk all day long. We spend the afternoon playing bridge. We stay indoors too much. We eat a hurried luncheon of highly refined foods which are lacking in bulk. We neglect regular toilet habits. Is there any wonder that a great majority of us suffer from constipation?

"New Way of Living," The Kellogg Company, 1932

Even peanut butter had to be invented. It started as a health food, developed by a doctor in St. Louis in 1890 as an easily digested high-protein product. It was a huge success—how could it not be? It wasn't just healthy; it tasted good. Grocers kept it in big tubs, stirring it up for customers before ladling it out.

Butter is man-made, though we don't usually think of it that way. Margarine is, in a manner of speaking, even more man-made than butter. It was invented in response to Napoleon III's offer of a handsome prize to whomever could find a way to produce "a cheap butter for the Army, Navy, and needy classes...." The resulting margarine (pronounced with a hard "g" in France) was made of suet mixed with milk and churned into solid fat. Later, the liquid oil—"oleine"—was

KERR SCREW BAND

KERR MASON LID
(WITH THE NATURAL GRAY SEALING
COMPOSITION FLOWED IN)

KERR MASON CAP (COMPLETE)

The Screw Band

Kerr Mason Lid

separated from the lard; the solid part was called "stearin" or "margarine," and the hard fat resulting was called "butterine." Later still, the liquid oleine was hardened by hydrogenation. Solid vegetable fats like Crisco were manufactured later as marvels of hygiene; they could be kept at room temperature almost forever.

Even tea bags have a place in the processed food procession. It was just past the turn of the twentieth century when a tea merchant, Thomas Sullivan, decided to send samples of his various blends to his customers. He devised little hand-sewn bags to hold the samples. The great leap was made by his customers, who discovered that they could put a bag in a cup and pour boiling water over it. That doesn't sound like much to us, but it was the gulf between a pot and a cup, and it was large. The customers ordered more tea—but now in tea bags.

Iced tea was equally accidental. Various people had cooled their own glasses of tea over the years, but it took the St. Louis International Exposition in 1904 to make it popular. It happened, according to the story, when the man with the tea booth realized no one was buying his tea because they were already too hot—the weather was steaming, just like the tea. In desperation, he put a chunk of ice in the tea urn. His iced tea was a sensation. (The St. Louis fair also gave us the ice cream cone—when the ice cream vendor ran out of dishes and another merchant saved the day by making instant cones out of the wafer cookies *he* was selling.)

There are those who say that hamburgers were put on a bun for the first time at that same St. Louis Fair in 1904. Hamburgers trace their name back to Germany; they travelled from Russia's Baltic provinces—where chopped beef was eaten raw—to Hamburg. The raw meat (called Steak Tartare) was cooked in Hamburg and eventually emigrated to America, where it became known as hamburger. Another favorite immigrant is the hot dog, which is known as a Frankfurter in Vienna and a wiener in Frankfurt. Hot dogs derive their name from a 1906 cartoon in which the German meat inside the long bun was a wiggling dachshund. Hot dogs are made of beef, pork, mutton, goat (yes, goat), chicken, or turkey, plus fat, cereal fillers, and preservatives.

By the turn of the century, food processing was big business, accounting, by itself, for 20% of all American manufacturing. The four largest areas of the food industry—meat packing, flour milling, sugar refining, and baked goods—were either already dominated by large corporations, or soon would be.

The Kitchen Liberation of Women

In the *Boston Cooking School Cook Book*, first published in 1896, Fannie Merritt Farmer put all these achievements together for the first time and moved them yet ahead a step. She brought science to cooking. There were no more "dashes" of this or "pieces" of that—a lump of butter as big as a walnut, or a handful of raisins. Fannie Farmer insisted on level, consistent measurement, and on accurate cooking temperatures as well.

JAPAN TEA

THE CUP THAT CHEERS.
"WELCOME" IN JAPAN
THE LAND OF
COLOR, COURTESY and CHARM

She believed that cooking was a precise art—that any dish could be reproduced in any kitchen, provided its recipe were as accurate as a scientific formula meant to be reproduced in a laboratory. It was this approach to food, coupled with advances in food preservation and preparation methods, that freed women from the hours of drudgery which had bound them to their coal stoves and wooden sinks as securely as if their apron strings had been tied around the faucets and handles as well as around their waists.

Every step in the path from ice house to ice box to refrigerator to freezer, from the open hearth to the self-cleaning oven, from packaged yeast to canned peaches, was a move towards the emancipation of women from the kitchen, and toward the art of cooking as well.

The turn of the twentieth century was when all these changes bubbled at their peak, before absurdity took over from the reason of convenience foods and imitation food boomed. After World War II, artificial tastes and flavor stretchers, stabilizers, and enhancers, made madness out of good sense. Until then, each new product maintained its integrity, filled a need, tasted *real*. Even canned food didn't become widespread until it was not only safe (everyone thought it caused ptomaine poisoning) but was also of good quality. Until then, housewives preserved food by pickling, salting, and smoking it, stewing it in sugar, drying it in the sun, or fermenting it. They didn't can it until they were sure it would taste good and it wouldn't give anyone a stomach ache.

Then the advertising and merchandising began.

Something different had happened to the business of food: It had always been the selling of available food to a hungry market. Now, the consumer had to be *convinced* to buy one kind of food rather than another. Where once the food business had meant growing food, transporting it, and selling it, at the turn of the last century the food business also began to mean processing food and marketing it. What had been a question of *filling* a demand was now a matter of *creating* a demand.

How do you create a demand? By selling an idea. By persuading and convincing. By advertising.

The Recipe Pamphlets

Some of the earliest food advertisements were the pamphlets published by the new companies. Taking a cue from Mrs. Knox's collection of recipes, reams of cooking booklets were issued, all showing how many ways one food product could be used. Especially if it were the right brand.

GETTING HIS OWN BREAKFAST

Shredded Wheat

Ready-Cooked — Ready-to-Eat

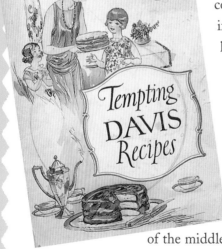

That was the idea behind the recipe pamphlets: They offered a thousand and one dishes, each using the same product, each created by an expert. They also showed the lady of the house how to use the new product—the magic powdered gelatin, the instant baking powder. They taught her how to cook, now that the kitchen maid had given notice and gone to work in the factory.

The result was to join kitchens from New York to San Francisco in a chain of Knox gelatin and Fleischmann's yeast, Rumford baking powder, Minute Tapioca, and Jell-O. Merchandising of convenience foods was the spoon that stirred the American melting pot when we still believed that melting was both possible and good. Golden Glow Salad was on the menu in Maine just as it was in Minnesota. You could have cottage pudding for dessert in Nashville or New York City. It was a pre-media nationalization of American culture.

The cooking pamphlets were used with good faith. People still believed that the result of hard work was happiness. Dinner would surely please if it were cooked with the best ingredients and with care, and if the family were well fed it would be healthy and happy and grateful to the cook. A well-run kitchen, a scientific diet, and dainty food could keep you safe. No demons could enter a house where a woman knew how to make a decent white sauce; no marriage could fail if Little Mrs. Bride knew how to bake a good cake.

The pamphlets also mark a time when American kitchens were passing from the majesty of the aristocracy to the homogeneity of the middle class. Finger bowls with leaves of rose geraniums floating in them were as impractical as the white gloves ladies wore to dinner. There would soon be no one around to pluck the geranium leaf or pass the finger bowl; no one wanted to spare the time to wash the gloves, which were removed and placed in the lap as soon as everyone had seen them, anyway. Servants had other, better, work to do. It was time for madam to learn how to cook.

The recipes provided by these miniature cook books were meant for beginning cooks as well as for the experienced cook who was ready to

try something new. They were easy to follow; they were often excellent; they were always devised by experts whose purpose it was to make a single product indispensible. It was the manufacturer's dream that housewives would follow his instructions and use his brand and then buy it happily ever after. (Their sweet, pure, simple minds would, of course, be uncorrupted by visions of his competitors' products.)

My brand is safe, they each said, and reliable, and they were usually right. My brand will make you happy, they each claimed, and thus they ventured onto more metaphysical ground.

Some of these pamphlets were the only cook-books their owners possessed, and they provided recipes for everything from a loaf of bread to frozen mousse. Many of the pamphlets ended up tucked in the pages of a larger and less parochial book, Fannie Farmer, perhaps, or stuffed into drawers or desk cubbies. Some of them came with a loop of string threaded through a hole in one corner so they could be hung from a kitchen nail near the stove.

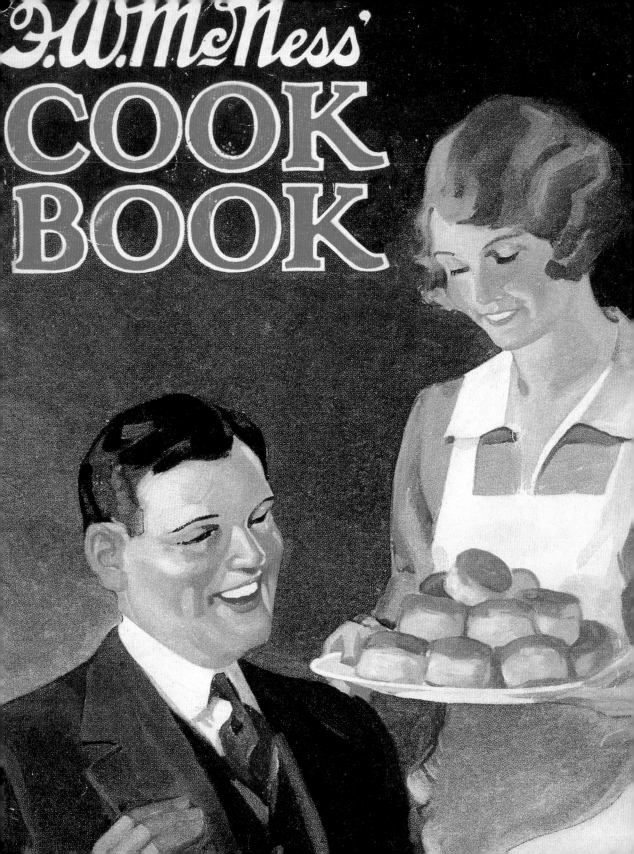

The recipes, like the booklets themselves, show a touching combination of naiveté and emerging sophistication. Every flour booklet has recipes for gems and biscuits, golden cake and sugar cookies, but there are also, popping up among the popovers, directions for making Spanish rice and Italian cream. These recipes reflect an increasing awareness of what the rest of the world eats for dinner. Wars and airplanes and television changed the American national food consciousness, but before these huge forces were in place, we were experimenting, in a timid way, with "Mexican Jelly Salad" and "Norwegian Canapés."

Food was amazingly bland in the first part of the twentieth century. These new dishes—chili con carne and "Goulasch as the Hungarian Shepherds Used to Make It"—were adventures, but they were not adventurous. The Goulash had a mere quarter-of-a-teaspoon of paprika in it.

They shall rise up and call her blessed—this woman who—loving and thoughtful of future joy and health—secures the goodness of Nature at her best, and cans against the barren sameness of the Winter months.

"Ball Blue Book," Ball Preserving, 1934

The French statesman and writer Talleyrand is supposed to have said England was a country with twenty-four religions and only one sauce. America was not very different. White sauce covered everything. It flowed from coast to coast, wherever there was a tablespoon of butter, another of flour, and a cup of milk. It was seasoned with salt and pepper. Period. Gradually, other ingredients crept in: lemon juice with fish, or a bit of cheese in a gratin. These were also the days when butter and milk and eggs and cream were good for you. Sugar, of course, was simply sweet.

Inevitably, things began to get more complicated. Exotic food began to arrive: pineapples and oranges and bananas. Recipe pamphlets introduced them, and showed us how to cook with them.

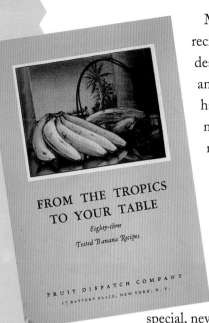

FROM THE TROPICS
TO YOUR TABLE
Eighty-three
Tested Banana Recipes

FRUIT DISPATCH COMPANY
17 BATTERY PLACE, NEW YORK, N. Y.

Manufacturers began to glamorize cooking itself. At first, recipe booklets were pamphlets for a revolution. In a way, they dealt with the common sense of the kitchen—how to cook and clean—and the rights of woman as cook. They might have been Tom Paine's, though, of course, their message was more muted. When those first battles had been won—now no one spent hours reducing beef broth to make gelatin—the merchandisers turned to face new scrimmages.

When there was no longer a need to convince women that a specific product could save them time and energy, the message changed: This product is more economical, or more nutritious, or more delicious. These are the values to be found in this package and not in that one. Knowing all this, the cook would be enveloped by a special, new kind of glow as she worked—a glow that still glimmers in food advertising today. The road from taste appeal to sex appeal is a very short one, as Adam and Eve taught us all.

Each product brought its vision of happiness into the kitchen. "They'll love you when you serve..." Even beyond this, cooking became a good deed that went past its first virtue of filling the stomach with appetizing food. Particular products could be counted on to taste better, to taste more real, to taste—even then!—more like mother's. And they had a monopoly on health. The virtuous struggle seemed always to be to get the food inside your loved ones; once there, the product could be counted on to turn into a barricade against the raging germs outside. There was no penicillin then, only chicken soup.

When all of this had succeeded—convenience, speed, domestic science, nourishment, and taste—the recipe pamphlets began to depend on glamour, for the kitchen, for the dining room, and for the woman who had made it all possible (with a little help from the secret package). It was not only that if she used the right brand she too would be glamorous. It was very much that the food itself should be part of the general striving for an ambiance of elegance and tone. Even the stars had to eat, after all. "Favorite Recipes of the Movie Stars" proved it. This booklet was much larger than most, as is only fitting, and it plugged breakfast, lunch, dinner, and the movies.

CHILI—AS IT WAS THEN

Here are two early recipes for chili. They both speak of the days when Spanish Rice was an exotic food. The first recipe has never heard of chili powder (not to mention cumin, oregano, chili peppers, or even salt and pepper). And it is to be served at an after-the-theater luncheon. Was theater then something you did BEFORE lunch? An early morning show, perhaps, followed by a bottle of catsup...

Fry a pound and a half of hamburger and one small onion, chopped, in large skillet until meat is cooked. Add a large bottle of catsup and cook until mixture appears oily. Then add a can of red kidney beans and allow to cook until mixture appears dry. Then serve.

This can be prepared and kept in the Frigidaire to be reheated when desired for serving.

It is a most acceptable Sunday night supper dish and makes a popular after-the-theater luncheon.

Six to eight servings
From "Your Frigidaire," Frigidaire, 1933

This second recipe is a little more advanced: it uses salt and pepper AND a quarter teaspoon of chili powder—IF DESIRED. The tomato comes from a can of tomato soup, instead of catsup.

Brown one pound ground beef in a skillet with one tablespoonful butter and a chopped onion. Add a medium can of Heinz Oven Baked Red Kidney Beans and stir until well blended. Pour over this a small can of Heinz Cream of Tomato Soup. Season, using one teaspoonful salt, a dash of pepper, and ¼ teaspoonful Chili Powder (if desired). Serve with boiled or baked potatoes or with boiled rice.

From "Savory Meat Dishes," Heinz, c. 1930

It may be well to remind the housewife that the Pure Food Laws of this nation do not guarantee the purity of food products. All they vouch for is that the food complies with the label outside.

"Delicious Desserts and Candies,"
Dr. Price's Vanilla Extract,
1923

Now the transition was complete; voyage done. The freezer was on the horizon and take-out food just down the pike. Modern women have come by their freedom in the kitchen through the cumulative effect of all these small and separate achievements. Technology in the bedroom—contraceptives—gave women a choice about how many babies to have and even when to have them. Technology in the kitchen—up to today's microwaves and frozen foods and everything we take for granted—gave women a choice about how to spend their days, now that their nights were secure.

Dinner used to grow in the garden. What couldn't be picked, plucked, or pickled was scarce and few could afford it. Today, the fortunate cook has a near infinity of ingredients from which to choose. Our kitchens are a triumph of technology, from the sleek, cool microwave to the least little no-stick frying pan.

What gets cooked in that kitchen is equally up-to-date: foods such as pre-cooked rice, pre-sliced carrots, pre-soaked beans, pre-shredded cole slaw.

The market place has become equally marvelous. Everything (from packaged salads to eighteen varieties of mustard) is all in one place, every day, and always the same.

But now we've learned not to be satisfied, even with mashed potato flakes and soup in microwavable cardboard cups. Everything

Partially Ripe Banana with green tip—The starch is not yet fully converted into sugar; in this condition bananas should not be eaten raw, but may be cooked in many tempting ways as a vegetable or a dessert.

Yellow Ripe Banana—All green color has disappeared and the pulp contains only a very small percentage of starch. The fruit now has a delicious flavor and can be readily digested by any healthy person.

Fully Ripe Banana flecked with brown—The banana is now at its best for flavor and nutrition. It may be eaten freely by everyone.

continues to simplify, concentrate, dehydrate, and—maybe—improve. The spin is to make everything faster and easier. There's only a small distance between tonight's dinner and the dinner of the future—a take-out little green pill?—but there's a vast space between shopping, cooking, and eating today and the kitchen of a hundred years ago.

Our great-grandparents ate by the calendar: strawberries in June, raspberries in July, tomatoes in August, apples in the fall, and jam in the winter. When they slaughtered a pig, they ate fresh meat. The rest of the time, there was salt pork. Life pivoted (as it always had) on the need to guarantee that there would be food for dinner. We've come so far from those days of necessary self-sufficiency, when each house had its own fruit trees, butter churn, vegetable garden, chicken coop, and cows in the barn, that living off the land, no longer a necessity, is now a fashion.

The cooking pamphlets are a reminder of what was. They're filled with simplicity and a kind of sweet innocence. They're full of hope and trust. Our present is their future. Their recipes are the flavors of our food heritage, a kitchen history of our family tree. These are our kitchen treasures.

*T*he majority of recipes included herein were selected by internationally famous food experts from the returns of a world-wide contest in which 121,619 housewives, here and abroad, competed.

"A Cook's Tour," Minute Tapioca, 1929

Starters, Soups, and Salads

Bermuda Relish Canapés

O ne of the canapés that made James Beard famous, when he began in the food business as a caterer, was his onion sandwich: rounds of thin slices of onion sandwiched, with mayonnaise, between rounds of brioche, the edges slathered with mayonnaise and then rolled in chopped parsley. These innocent Bermuda Relish bits must be kin, like a cousin once-removed, from a generation or so earlier. In other words, they got there first. They're oniony, but the end result is not as sharp as you might expect. The sweeter and milder the onion, of course, the sweeter and milder the Bermuda Relish. Try Vidalias, in season (they're really barely onions at all) or red onions—and even those benighted souls who don't love onions will find these canapés hard to resist.

6 slices of white bread, crusts removed
(Use a good bread or, even better, a small brioche, a brioche loaf, or challah)
1 to 2 tablespoons sweet butter, at room temperature

¼ pound cream cheese, at room temperature
6 thin slices of red or Vidalia onion, quartered

1. Toast the bread on one side and spread the untoasted side lightly with butter.
2. Spread half the cream cheese over the buttered side. Quarter each slice.
3. Top each toast quarter with a quartered onion slice.
4. Spread the remaining cream cheese over the onion slices. (It helps to hold the onion down with one finger.)
5. Just before serving, preheat the oven to 350 degrees. Bake the toasts on a cookie sheet until the cheese is slightly browned, about 10 minutes.

Note: If you feel strongly that butter *and* cream cheese is just too much fat, leave out the butter.

Serves 6 to 8

Adapted from "Cheese Recipes"
Baumert Cheese, c. 1925-1935

Cheese Canapés

*F*or years, cookbooks often included a recipe that called for a mixture of cream cheese, blue cheese, butter, and Cognac, to spread on crackers. We actually used to eat that way! (And it was delicious.) This recipe, which dates to the 1920s, may be that rich combination's antecedent. It leaves out the butter, and cuts the richness of the cheese with a bit of tomato. The pamphlet version calls for sherry, but I prefer to include as a choice, in honor of the cheese and crackers I once enjoyed, the same old Cognac.

¼ pound cream cheese (about ½ cup—
   half of an 8-ounce package)
3 tablespoons Roquefort cheese
½ teaspoon Worcestershire sauce
1 teaspoon Cognac, Sherry, or milk
¼ teaspoon sweet paprika
6 slices of good white bread, crusts removed
12 thin slices of tomato

1. Blend the cream cheese with the Roquefort. (A food processor is the fastest way to do this.)
2. Add the Worcestershire, Cognac, and paprika, and blend well.
3. Cut the bread in quarters or rounds. Toast on one side.
4. Spread the untoasted sides with the cheese mixture, and top each with a slice of tomato.
   (If you have cut the bread into quarters, do the same with the tomatoes.)

Serves 6 to 8

Adapted from "Cheese Recipes"
Baumert Cheese, c. 1925-1935

Florida Spread

When George Washington was a lad—19 years old, in 1752—he traveled to Barbados with his brother, Lawrence, who had been told he needed to recover from a recent illness in a warm climate. George sampled the native fruits. He wrote about grapefruit, called Shaddock after the English sea captain who had brought the seeds from Polynesia, and his personal favorite, pineapple ("none pleases my taste as do's the pine"), and the fruit he noted as especially abundant and most popular among the locals, the "agovado."

Agovados—otherwise known as avocados—traveled to Florida in 1833 when a local horticulturist planted the Mexican variety on his land south of Miami. The century was to change yet again before avocados became commercially successful in the early 1900s.

This recipe was proudly published in 1933 to spotlight the wonders of the modern refrigerator. The pamphlet notes that it should be "served extremely cold as you may so easily do by chilling it in your Westinghouse refrigerator for an hour."

1 avocado, peeled
1 cup crab meat, picked over to remove
   cartilage and filaments
pinch of salt
freshly ground black pepper to taste

SOUR CREAM DRESSING:
   ½ cup sour cream
   1 teaspoon vinegar
   ¼ teaspoon salt
   2 teaspoons lemon juice
   dash of cayenne pepper

1. Mash the avocado (leaving it a bit lumpy) and mix with the crab meat, salt, and pepper.
2. Combine the ingredients for the sour cream dressing and stir the dressing, gently but thoroughly, into the avocado mixture. Chill. Serve as a spread for crackers or bread, or as a dip for vegetables.

Serves 4 to 6

Adapted from "The Refrigerator Book"
Westinghouse, 1933

Ginger Toasts

James Kraft came to the United States from Canada in 1904. He used some of his small savings to buy a horse and a wagon; with his remaining capital of $65, he started a cheese delivery service. Five years later, he founded J. L. Kraft Bros. in partnership with his accountant and his brothers; together they invested $15,000. The first year, Kraft lost $3,000 plus his horse. He persevered, introduced new pasteurizing processes and packaged cheeses, and, as we all know, eventually prospered. Along the way, he bought the Phenix Cheese Company, producer of Philadelphia brand cream cheese. This company was founded by farmers to replace the Empire cheese plant after that factory burned down. "Phenix" was supposed to be "phoenix," the bird that rises triumphantly from ashes to live again, but the farmers spelled it wrong. No matter. Kraft Philadelphia brand *is* cream cheese. That's triumph.

> Butter that fails to come after the customary amount of churning will be hastened by a teaspoonful of The Great Arm & Hammer Soda.
>
> "Book of Valuable Recipes" Arm & Hammer, 1915

8 ounces cream cheese, at room temperature   2 tablespoons minced candied ginger

1. Blend the cream cheese and the ginger until smooth. (If necessary, add a bit of milk to make the mixture smooth and creamy.)

Yield: just over ½ cup

Note: This is especially good made ahead (and refrigerated); the ginger almost melts into the cream cheese. Feel free to add more ginger if you like, but don't overwhelm the cream cheese or your guests. It makes a lovely spread for toast or crackers, and it's awfully good with tea. It can be garnished, if you like, with chopped toasted almonds or walnuts.

Adapted from "The Refrigerator Book"
Westinghouse, 1933

Toast with Olive Oil and Cheese

*T*his recipe is from a pamphlet that features dishes from "World Famous Chefs of the United States, Canada, and Europe," with photographs and biographical notes for each. ("Jules Dauviller, chef de cuisine at the Palace Hotel, was formerly the $10,000 a year dictator of the cuisine [*sic*] in the home of Mr. and Mrs. Harry Payne Whitney in New York. The Whitneys got him from the Grand Hotel in Paris." Yes, that's correct, he was the *dictator* of the cuisine. And they paid him.)

The chefs worked in hotels from Cape May to Dresden, and they volunteered an equally wide range of recipes. Frozen pineapple with kirschwasser, Salade Ecossaise ("Choose six nice celery roots..."), Caviar Romanoff, pickled walnuts, and Maiden's Blush Appetizer (toast topped with lobster salad, caviar in a scooped-out hard boiled egg, and sliced pimento) are just a tiny sampling.

Toast with Olive Oil and Cheese is very much like what we would now call bruschetta—slices of Italian bread brushed with garlic and olive oil and baked with a variety of toppings.

4 slices of Italian bread

1 tablespoon extra-virgin olive oil

¼ cup Parmesan cheese (use a type such
   as Parmigiano-Reggiano, and grate it yourself)

freshly ground black pepper

lemon juice

1. Preheat the oven to 350 degrees.
2. Brush each slice of bread generously with olive oil. Sprinkle with the cheese, a few grinds of black pepper, and a few drops of lemon juice. Place on a baking sheet.
3. Bake until the cheese melts and the bread is lightly browned, about 5 minutes. Serve immediately.

Note: If you'd like a garlicky flavor, toast the bread lightly first, rub each slice with a halved clove of garlic, and then continue.

The mystery chef who contributed this recipe (his signature is illegible) suggests an alternative: mash anchovies with an equal quantity of butter, add chopped parsley and spread over lightly toasted bread in a thin layer. Other possible toppings: chopped tomatoes, onion, and basil marinated in a garlicky vinaigrette; chopped mushrooms mixed with minced onion, a bit of mashed garlic, oil and vinegar; or chopped olives, minced garlic and chopped parsley mixed with oil and vinegar. Use good Italian bread.

Adapted from "Ultra Select Dishes
for Afternoon Teas"
International Publishing Co., 1913

Wakimoli

Y ou probably thought guacamole came from Mexico! In "Favorite Recipes of the Movie Stars," published in 1931, Helen Twelvetrees called this recipe Wakimoli, which makes it sound as if it came from Hawaii.

Ms. Twelvetrees (whose real name was Helen Jurgens) starred in a series of tear-filled movies in the late twenties and the thirties, but her recipe is quite joyful. It has the blandness of the food of her time, but here, the blandness—no chili powder, no garlic, no lime juice, and of course, no cilantro—is a kind of blessing, because what you end up with is a very intense avocado flavor. It's delicious. And it's kept fresh and green by the mayonnaise, even more lavish in the original recipe, which called for a full cup.

2 ripe avocados
½ small onion, chopped fine
¼ cup mayonnaise plus
    1 tablespoon (regular or low fat)
salt and freshly ground black
    pepper to taste
pinch of sweet paprika
garnish (optional): a sprinkle of
    chili powder

1. Scoop out the avocados and mash (use a fork or a food processor) until only a bit lumpy.
2. Add the onion, ¼ cup of mayonnaise, and seasonings.
3. Pile the Wakimoli into a glass serving dish—the color is so pale and pretty!—and spread a thin layer of mayonnaise, using the additional tablespoon, across the top to ensure that it will stay green.

Note: Serve as a spread with crackers or corn chips, use to stuff endive leaves, spread on bread and add thinly sliced onions for a wonderful sandwich, or pile in the center of a salad plate and surround with sliced tomatoes, onions and black olives. If you'd like a small reminder of authenticity and roots, sprinkle with a bit of chili powder.

Yield: about one cup

Adapted from "Favorite Recipes of the Movie Stars," 1931

Cream of Onion Soup

When you think of onion soup, inevitably you think of French onion soup—onion slices simmered in a rich beef broth, topped with sliced French bread and blanketed liberally with cheese, and then baked until the cheese and bread are crusty.

This onion soup is different. It won't replace the other—why should it?—but it stands wonderfully well on its own. It's a *comforting* kind of soup, and that's a very special quality. It has a rich, nutritious flavor, naturally sweet from the onions and the milk. I think it should stand in the first rank of comfort food.

The other onion soup, a late night favorite at the old French market, is actually Polish. It was brought to the court of Louis XV by the king's father-in-law, the deposed King Stanislaus of Poland. He also invented *baba au rhum*, the sweet, spongy cake soaked in rum syrup.

Cream of Onion Soup is not as sophisticated or as continental as French/Polish Onion Soup. It's simple, honest, and good, and that's plenty.

2 medium onions, chopped	½ teaspoon salt
2 tablespoons butter	3 cups milk (fresh whole or skim, or
1 cup chicken or vegetable broth	evaporated whole or skim diluted in
2 tablespoons rice	an equal amount of water)

1. Cook the onions in the butter until they are translucent. (Don't let them brown. They should be soft and golden.)
2. Add the broth, rice, and salt and cook for 15 minutes, or until the rice is tender.
3. Add the milk, bring back to the simmer, and taste to see if additional salt is needed.

Serves 4

Adapted from "Rice—200 Delightful Ways to Serve It"
Southern Rice Industry, 1935

Cold Mushroom Soup

*T*his is an unusual and subtle jellied soup, cooling on a hot day. The relatively new electric refrigerators were hitting their stride in the 1930s—with their tiny freezer sections for ice cubes, and their Art Deco coils on top—and a jellied soup, once so difficult and time-consuming to prepare, was a mark of luxury and glamour. Be sure the seasonings are sufficient for a cold soup; you may want to add a bit of lemon juice while the broth is hot to point up the flavor.

4 teaspoons unflavored gelatin
1/4 cup plus 1 1/2 cups water
3/4 pound mushrooms, cleaned and sliced
1 1/2 cups chicken broth (homemade or low sodium)
3 thick slices of onion

1 stalk celery with top
salt and freshly ground black pepper
garnish: a sprig of parsley or watercress, or a dollop of sour cream or yogurt

1. Sprinkle the gelatin over the 1/4 cup of water and let it sit for about 5 minutes. (Use a heat-proof cup.)

2. Place the mushrooms in a medium saucepan. Add the remaining 1 1/2 cups of water, all of the chicken broth, the onion, celery, and salt and pepper to taste. Bring to a boil, lower the heat, and cook over gentle heat for 20 minutes. Strain, pressing on the solids to extract as much liquid as possible.

3. Dissolve the gelatin by placing it, in its cup, in a saucepan. Add enough hot water to the saucepan to come up the side of the cup just to the level of the gelatin. Place the pan over low heat, and stir the gelatin, which will begin to dissolve. When it has completely dissolved, stir it into the mushroom broth. Taste for seasoning and adjust as necessary. Refrigerate for at least 2 hours.

4. Garnish with a sprig of parsley or watercress, or a dollop of sour cream or yogurt.

Serves 4 to 6

Adapted from "The Silent Hostess
Treasure Book"
GE Refrigerators, 1930

Hamburg Vegetable Soup

*T*hink hamburger, and you picture that meaty circle on a bun, symbol of the hungry American at home and abroad. One theory traces hamburger's heritage back to Russia's Baltic provinces, where there was a taste for raw beef, finely chopped and well seasoned. From there, what we now call Steak Tartare migrated across the Baltic Sea to the German port of Hamburg, where eventually and inevitably, some enterprising cook tried cooking the raw meat. It was only a question of time before Hamburg steak, née Steak Tartare, crossed the Atlantic, met its destiny inside a soft roll, and was named for the home it had left behind, like many immigrants.

A marvelous use for the well-traveled hamburger meat (in 1934 still called Hamburg) is this rich and surprising soup. It tastes as if it had been simmering all day instead of just for an hour. It's both robust and very easy to make—and fast, because it's based on hamburger instead of soup meat and a marrow bone. Use good chopped meat—sirloin, round, or the packaged additive-free chopped meat; there will be less fat, and the soup will taste even better.

1 tablespoon butter
1 medium onion, chopped
2 medium carrots, diced
½ cup diced celery (2 or 3 stalks)
¾ pound ground beef—sirloin or
   low fat
1½ quarts water
2 cups canned tomatoes, crushed or
   chopped

2 cups potatoes, cubed (it isn't
   necessary to peel the potatoes, but
   do scrub them)
½ cup rice or barley
1 cup peas, fresh or frozen
salt and freshly ground black pepper
   to taste
garnish: chopped parsley

1. Melt the butter in a soup pot and sauté the onion for about 5 minutes. Add the carrots and celery and continue to cook over low heat, stirring occasionally, until the onion is soft and translucent.
2. Add the meat and, using a wooden spoon to break it apart, cook until it is no longer red.
3. Add the water, tomatoes (with their juice), and the potatoes. If using barley, add it now.
4. Bring the soup to a boil, lower the heat, and simmer for 30 minutes.
5. If using rice, add it now and continue to simmer for another 15 to 30 minutes.
6. About 10 minutes before you plan to serve the soup, add the peas and salt and pepper to taste. If fat has pooled on the surface, skim off as much as you can. Serve hot, garnished with chopped parsley.

Serves 6

Adapted from "Meat Selection and Preparation"
Armour Meat, 1934

Hindu Soup

No doubt the Minute Tapioca Company called this soup "Hindu" because it contains curry powder, though an almost infinitesimal quarter-teaspoon was in the original 1928 recipe. Curry powder was still exotic then, and American food was still quite bland.

Tapioca was exotic too, once. Its more widespread use was part of the kitchen revolution that accompanied the industrial revolution, though a bit later. Around the turn of the century, a sailor brought back to a Boston boardinghouse tales of South Sea natives pounding tapioca (derived from the tropical cassava plant) in mortars to make it easier to use. He told the cook to put her tapioca through a coffee grinder so it wouldn't lump; she did, it worked, and she started selling it to her neighbors. Soon she was calling her product "Minute Tapioca." It was the first packaged food to add the virtue of speed to that of convenience.

This soup has all those virtues: it's exotic (well, a little), it's convenient, and it's quickly made. And it's delicious.

1 small onion, chopped
1 tart apple (such as Granny Smith), peeled, cored, and chopped
1 tablespoon butter
½ teaspoon dry mustard
1 teaspoon curry powder
½ teaspoon sugar

2 cups canned tomatoes, crushed
4 cups chicken or vegetable broth
3 tablespoons Minute Tapioca
salt and freshly ground black pepper to taste (the broth may already be salted; taste carefully)

1. Cook the onion and apple in the butter until the onion is soft and translucent. Stir in the mustard, curry powder, and sugar, and continue to cook for 2 or 3 minutes. Add the tomatoes and simmer for 20 minutes.
2. Add the broth and bring to a boil. Lower the heat and stir in the tapioca. Cook, stirring frequently for 15 minutes or until the tapioca is clear. Season to taste.

Serves 6

Adapted from "From Soup to Dessert"
Minute Tapioca, 1928

Navy Bean Soup

The 1945 edition of "The Cook Book of the Stars," published by WFBL, a CBS network radio station in Syracuse, New York, was published in wartime; its cover is red, white, and blue. Many CBS radio stars—singers, comedians, journalists, actors—contributed recipes to the pamphlet. Each recipe is really a double plug: one for the radio program and one for its sponsor. In those days, programs were presented by one advertiser, and stars were very much identified with their sponsor's product.

"The First Line," sponsored by Wrigley's Gum, is one of the programs featured in the pamphlet. Its star, though, wasn't a radio personality. "This series of exciting half-hour programs," reads the pamphlet copy, "has one hero, the United States Navy.... Prepared in close cooperation with the Navy, this series brings to the nation a new understanding of the magnitude and achievements of the Navy, a surging pride in the men of the naval service, and a firm confidence in the high quality of Navy leadership."

Maybe they chose Navy Bean Soup to represent the Navy just because they loved it. On the other hand, it isn't called Army Bean Soup.

1½ cups dried navy beans	½ teaspoon thyme
water for soaking	6 cups water
1 smoked ham bone (see Note)	½ cup half and half, whole milk, or
2 carrots, diced	undiluted evaporated skim milk
2 stalks celery, diced	¾ teaspoon sugar
1 medium onion, diced	salt and freshly ground black pepper
2 tablespoons chopped parsley	to taste

1. Rinse the beans, discarding small pebbles. Soak overnight in water that covers them by 3 inches, or bring the beans and water to a boil, simmer for 2 minutes, remove from the heat, and let stand for 1 hour. Drain.
2. Place the drained beans in a soup pot and add the ham bone, vegetables, parsley, thyme, and the 6 cups of water. Bring to a boil, reduce the heat, and let simmer until the beans are soft, about 2 hours.
3. Force the beans through a sieve, or purée in a food processor. Add the half and half, sugar, and salt and pepper. Heat gently until hot, stirring often.

Note: The pamphlet notes that you may substitute 4 strips of bacon for the ham bone. The soup is also delicious without any meat at all.

Serves 6

Adapted from "The Cook Book of the Stars"
WFBL, Columbia Broadcasting System Network, 1945

Peanut Butter Cream Soup

"Peanut Butter," says "Helpful Suggestions," a pamphlet published by J. W. Beardsley's Sons in 1927, "has in recent years been raised to a place of prominence in the list of foods. It contains a very large percentage of protein, vitamines and fat, and is not only a favorite with children, but is easy of digestion and assimilation. It is considered an almost perfect food."

Yes. There's more protein in peanuts, by weight, than there is in steak. They're high in the B vitamins, especially niacin and thiamin, and they're a good source of phosphorous. They're inexpensive, portable, and stay fresh for a remarkably long time. And they smoosh into peanut butter.

All of this makes Peanut Butter Cream Soup rather special. It does have a high fat content (once definitely an asset), but it's mostly unsaturated. With a salad, bread, and fruit for dessert, it makes a satisfying meal.

In the original Beardsley recipe, everything was steeped in the milk, which was then strained and stirred into a butter-flour roux. I think it's more satisfying this way. Use creamy or chunky peanut butter, but chunky has a single great advantage: all those chunks. I like that texture in the final dish.

2 tablespoons butter	4 cups milk
1 small onion, chopped	1 bay leaf
3 stalks celery, chopped	salt and freshly ground black
½ teaspoon paprika	pepper to taste
2 tablespoons flour	½ cup peanut butter

1. Melt the butter in a saucepan and sauté the onions and celery until they are soft and the onions are translucent. Add the paprika and flour, and cook, stirring, for 3 minutes.
2. Whisk in the milk and stir well, scraping up any bits on the bottom of the pan. Add the bay leaf and cook over low heat for 10 minutes, stirring often.
3. Stir in the peanut butter. It melts into the soup as you stir. Season to taste, remove the bay leaf, and serve.

Serves 4

Adapted from "Beardsley's Helpful Suggestions"
J. W. Beardsley's Sons, 1927

Tomato Soup

*I*n 1893, the United States Supreme Court established, for trade purposes, that tomatoes could be classified as a vegetable, even though tomatoes are really a fruit. I wonder how we would feel about tomatoes if we thought of them as fruits. Would our taste for them fried, baked, stewed, in sandwiches, sauces, and soups remain the same?

Tomato soup is an old stand-by. Making it this way—with a white sauce—gives it a solid, satisfying, old-fashioned taste. White sauce covered the country once, oozing from coast to coast. When it was ubiquitous, it must have been tiresome. Today, just once in a while, it's rich and savory. Use a whisk and you won't have lumps.

The pamphlet instructs the cook to strain the tomatoes before adding them to the white sauce. Puréeing them in a food processor updates the procedure and gives the soup a lovely texture.

4 tablespoons butter
3 tablespoons flour
1 cup evaporated milk
½ cup plus ¾ cup water
salt and freshly ground black
    pepper to taste

2 cups canned tomatoes
1 thick slice onion
1 stalk celery, with leaves
1 teaspoon sugar
½ teaspoon salt
⅛ teaspoon sweet paprika

1. Melt the butter in a saucepan. Stir in the flour and cook for 3 minutes, stirring frequently. Whisk in the milk and ½ cup water and cook, whisking, until thickened. Season with salt and pepper.
2. In a separate pan, cook the tomatoes, ¾ cup water, onion, celery, sugar, and seasonings for 20 minutes, stirring from time to time. Process in small batches.
3. Slowly whisk the tomato mixture into the white sauce. Heat gently until hot. Taste for seasoning and adjust if necessary.

Serves 6

Adapted from "Ten Cooking Tests"
Borden's, 1927

Beet Aspic

*T*omato aspic may be old-fashioned, but beet aspic is up-to-date. It's a beautiful deep scarlet color—it glistens. Show off its color in a glass bowl, if you have one. It's much easier to spoon aspic from a bowl than it is to unmold and slice it, though when this pamphlet was published, that would have been unthinkable.

The pamphlet calls for using fresh beets, but if you do, you'll lose the beautiful scarlet color so easily achieved by using the liquid from the canned beets. Beet aspic goes very nicely with pork or fish—the taste is much like that of pickled beets.

1 15-ounce can beets, whole, chunked, sliced, or julienned—reserve the liquid
1½ tablespoons unflavored gelatin
¼ cup water
½ cup white vinegar
½ cup sugar

1 bay leaf
½ teaspoon mustard seed
½ teaspoon celery seed
salt and freshly ground black pepper to taste

1. Place the beets in a glass serving bowl.
2. Sprinkle the gelatin over the water in a small container and let sit for 5 minutes, until it is softened.
3. Place ¾ cup of the reserved beet liquid (add water if you don't have enough) in a saucepan, and add the vinegar, sugar, bay leaf, mustard seed, celery seed, and salt and pepper. Heat until the sugar is dissolved. Add the gelatin and stir until it is completely dissolved.
4. Let the mixture cool until it's safe to pour over the beets in the glass bowl. Remove and discard the bay leaf. Place the aspic in the refrigerator for 4 hours or until set.

Serves 6

Adapted from "New Salads"
Colman's Mustard, 1928

Brewster Asparagus Salad

*I*n 1927, the makers of Premier Pure Food Products (canned foods) published a collection of recipes that, they wrote, "have been coming to us for years." It wasn't easy, they noted, to decide which recipes to include. "We wish that it were possible to publish every one," they said. "Of course, that would be an expensive undertaking and would take a very long time." They chose the recipes they considered most unusual. Miss Carrie E. Owen, who is credited with the recipe for Brewster Salad, was a resident of Shamokin, Pennsylvania. In a perfect world, she would have lived in Brewster.

1 hard-cooked egg white, chopped
1 tablespoon India relish
1 tablespoon finely chopped parsley
2 tablespoons chopped canned pimiento or
    freshly roasted red peppers
salt and freshly ground black pepper to taste
2 tablespoons mayonnaise, or a vinaigrette
    made with 2 tablespoons salad oil and
    1 tablespoon wine vinegar
1 pound fresh asparagus, cooked and cooled,
    or 1 15-ounce can of asparagus

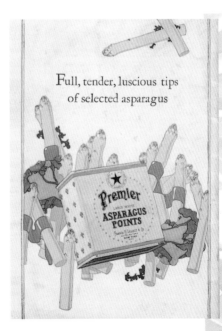

Full, tender, luscious tips
of selected asparagus

1. Mix egg white, relish, parsley, pimento, and salt and pepper. Stir in the mayonnaise.
2. Place the asparagus on a serving dish and criss-cross it with lines of the dressing.

Serves 4

Adapted from "Aladdin's Lamp at Mealtimes"
Premier Pure Food Products, 1927

Golden Wax Bean Salad

A letter to "The Housekeeper" is featured at the beginning of the Burt Olney Canning Company's 1909 pamphlet. "Dear Madam," it begins, "Few women appreciate the possibilities of canned goods." That's partly because in 1909, canned goods were still not yet always totally safe. But the pamphlet is filled with reassurances, and sweetness, and clarity. I would trust a can of Burt Olney's beans. On the other hand, the company seems to blame the very housewives it's trying to persuade. "(Women) use (canned goods) under protest and serve them with an apology. If this is true in your case, it is because you buy indiscriminately and serve what you buy in the old stereotyped way." The letter goes on to reassure us that Olney's canned goods satisfy the government's requirements for purity; and "they will satisfy you as to flavor."

This waxed bean salad can be made with fresh beans. It can also be made—without apology!—with canned beans. Just don't buy your beans indiscriminately. And if you get tired of waxed beans, you can make the same deliciously stereotyped salad with green beans—or, for that matter, almost any vegetable from asparagus to zucchini.

1 15-ounce can wax beans, drained, or 1 pound fresh beans, cooked and cooled
2 tablespoons red wine vinegar
4 tablespoons olive oil
2 tablespoons minced onion
1 small clove garlic, minced or crushed
1 to 2 tablespoons chopped parsley
freshly ground black pepper to taste

1. Combine the beans with the remaining ingredients. (Unless you buy low-sodium beans, they will already be salted, so taste carefully before adding more.)
2. Let stand for about an hour before serving to give the flavors a chance to meld.

Serves 4

Adapted from "Soups, Salads, and Desserts"
The Burt Olney Canning Co., 1909

Russian Salad

*I*n Russia, Russian Salad is called Salade Olivier. That's its formal name, and it is a formal salad. It was supposedly devised by a French chef named Olivier, employed by Czar Nicholas II at the Winter Palace. Come the revolution, Nicholas didn't fare too well, but Olivier escaped and made his way to Berlin, where he opened a restaurant. He probably served a wicked salad.

Salads that are called "Russian" usually have caviar in them. The most elegant way to serve this salad is in a pyramid shape or a mound with a dollop of caviar on the top, but it's fine without the caviar, too. I've had it in Russian restaurants served very simply in a bowl.

Exact quantities don't matter for this flexible salad, and neither do you have to use precisely these vegetables, though the salad almost always includes potatoes.

3 cups cooked vegetables, cubed—any or all of these: carrots, cauliflower, peas, celery, string beans, potatoes, beets, asparagus

1 cup cubed cooked chicken or ham (or a combination)

¼ cup dill pickle, cubed

½ cup mayonnaise or as much as is needed to coat the vegetables

salt and freshly ground black pepper

optional: chopped dill

garnish: tomatoes, cucumber, hard boiled eggs, black olives, sprigs of dill

1. Combine the vegetables, meat, pickle, and mayonnaise and mix well. Add the seasonings and adjust to taste as neccessary. Refrigerate until ready to serve.
2. Serve on lettuce leaves, garnished as you prefer—for example, with dill sprigs and tomato, cucumber, hard boiled egg wedges, and black olives.

Note: You may wish to marinate the vegetables in a vinaigrette dressing made with olive oil and wine vinegar. In that case, be sure they're well drained before mixing the salad with the mayonnaise.

Serves 6

Adapted from "The Sunday American Cook Book"
The Boston Sunday American, 1911

Perfection Salad

*I*t isn't perfect. It's cole slaw—sort of—and it goes back to the beginnings of powdered gelatin (one of the first of the industrial revolution's processed foods). Perfection Salad, wildly popular once, was part of two trends. The first was to make gelatin molds out of everything, even cole slaw, because using gelatin was newly easy and had status: You had to be able to provide the chill, and that meant you had an ice box. The second trend was to keep food neat and clean—"dainty" was the word—dainty on the plate, and prepared by the little woman, as opposed to the big chunky maid.

In that tradition, Perfection Salad was devised by Mrs. John E. Cooke of New Castle, Pennsylvania, who entered her recipe in a contest sponsored by Charles Knox in 1905. One of the judges was Fannie Farmer. Mrs. Cooke (felicitous name!) won third prize, a sewing machine.

The thing is, Perfection Salad is good. I'm not a fan of molded food unmolded—it always seems an unnecessary bother to me, fuss for the sake of fuss—but this is a lovely looking gelatin, and if you're willing to go through the process of unmolding, you will be very well rewarded. The original recipe, in an undated Knox pamphlet, suggests cutting the salad into cubes and serving it in cases made of the shells of red or green peppers. I wouldn't go that far—using pepper shells—but I do like the idea of letting the salad jell in a square baking dish, and then cubing it, and piling the cubes on a serving dish.

And if it isn't perfect—well, what is? Perfection Salad turns out to be, at least, very good.

2 tablespoons unflavored gelatin	½ teaspoon salt
½ cup cold water	1 cup finely shredded cabbage
½ cup boiling water	1 cup finely chopped or sliced celery
¼ cup sugar	¼ cup chopped red bell pepper
½ cup white or cider vinegar	freshly ground black pepper to taste
2 tablespoons lemon juice	

1. Sprinkle the gelatin over the cold water and let it sit for about 5 minutes until softened. Add the boiling water, sugar, vinegar, lemon juice and salt and stir until the gelatin is dissolved. Refrigerate.

2. When this mixture has begun to thicken and is syrupy, add the cabbage, celery, red pepper, and ground black pepper. Taste for salt and add more if necessary. Pour into a mold or bowl. (If the salad is to be served unmolded, rinse the mold with cold water and pour the mixture into the wet mold. A square baking dish can also be used and should also be rinsed and left wet.) Refrigerate for several hours.

3. Either serve from the bowl or unmold it by dipping the mold quickly into hot water, covering it with a serving dish, and in one fast motion, reversing so that the dish is on the bottom. Give it a firm shake and remove the mold. If it doesn't unmold, either dip it again in hot water or wrap the mold for a minute in a dish towel that has been dipped in hot water and quickly wrung out, and then try again. To serve cubes, dip the baking dish quickly into hot water. Cut the cubes with a sharp knife, run the knife around the sides to loosen them, and remove the cubes with a spatula.

Serves 6

Adapted from "Food Economy"
Knox Gelatin, c. 1905

Potato and Pimiento Salad

I love potato salad, and I like picnics a lot too. They go awfully well together, but then, potato salad goes with most things, anytime, anywhere.

Even love. Potatoes were once considered potent aphrodisiacs. "Eating of these roots doth excite Venus and increaseth lust," wrote one seventeenth-century writer. As luck would have it, many foods have been thought to be aphrodisiacs at one time or another, by one people or another. Pimientos have. So have eggs. This recipe includes potatoes, pimientos, and eggs, making, just possibly, for a nice, lusty salad. Of course, it's really not so much what you're eating as whom you're eating it with. My advice: Take a lover on a picnic and have some potato salad. After all, if nothing else, at least you'll have had a good meal. Together.

More advice, given to me once at a platonic Fourth of July picnic, and I pass it on here: The best potato salads have hard boiled eggs in them. That's the secret.

6 large boiling potatoes, scrubbed

2 canned pimientos, cubed, or 1 red pepper, cubed

4 tablespoons vegetable oil

2 tablespoons cider vinegar

2 tablespoons minced parsley

2 tablespoons minced onion

2 hard-boiled eggs, chopped

salt and freshly ground black pepper

4 tablespoons mayonnaise

1. Put the potatoes in a pot, cover them with lightly salted water, bring to a boil, and cook until tender when pierced with a knife. Drain. If you have an electric range, put the pot back on the hot burner until the remaining moisture has evaporated. Otherwise, put a folded towel over the potatoes, cover, and let sit for a few minutes—the towel will absorb the moisture.

2. While the potatoes are still warm, slice them. (Peeled or unpeeled is up to you. Sometimes, I partially peel them so the salad won't taste too strongly of peel.) Place them in a large bowl. Add the oil and vinegar, stir gently, and let stand for one hour. Stir in the remaining ingredients.

3. Taste to adjust the seasonings. You might want to add more onion, salt, pepper, or mayonnaise. Keep refrigerated until ready to serve.

The best cook will fail to furnish us with an acceptable dish if we have no appetite; but with a good appetite, any dish is welcome. "Hunger is the cook's best friend."

"Ayer's Preserve Book," Ayer's, 1898

Serves 6

Adapted from "Every Day Cooking for the Housekeeper and Student" Rumford Baking Powder, c. 1885

CERESOTA
COOK BOOK

*B*read is toasted to extract the moisture and make it more palatable and digestible.

To make toast, use stale bread, or dry slices in oven before toasting. Cut bread thin, about one-quarter of an inch, have fire red, not blazing. The crusts may be removed or not, according to

Breads

taste. Use double broiler, place slices in evenly, close broiler and hold firmly to prevent slices from slipping. Move gently over fire one or two minutes, turn over, then hold nearer to coals and brown. Serve at once, buttered or dry.

Bread properly toasted turns the dough into pure wheat farina, easily digested even by sick persons.

Always toast over coals or in oven.

"65 Delicious Dishes," Fleischmann's Yeast, 1919

Cinnamon Toast

Cinnamon goes way back. The first written mention of it was in a paper ascribed to a Chinese Emperor in 2700 B.C. For a long time, only small amounts of cinnamon reached Europe from the East, and it remained expensive, literally worth its weight in gold.

Today, we use cinnamon liberally, in dozens of ways, from mom's apple pie to the dusting on the top of a cup of cappuccino. Of all the things we can do with a little jar of cinnamon, one of the simplest—and most appealing, if we forget how humble it is—is cinnamon toast. Cinnamon toast is often associated with childhood, and it *is* full of innocence and purity. It is also sophisticated in its way, and incredibly dependable, always easily conjured up when the last cookie is gone. It's one of those things—so quiet, so honorable, so trustworthy, such a good sport—that we often forget it's there. Our loss. Cinnamon Toast is good.

6 slices white bread	⅓ cup sugar
¼ cup butter, at room temperature	1 tablespoon cinnamon

1. Preheat the broiler.
2. In the broiler, toast the bread on one side, watching carefully to be sure it doesn't scorch.
3. Cream the butter and the sugar; mix in the cinnamon.
4. Spread the butter mixture on the *untoasted* side of each bread slice.
5. Place the slices on a cookie sheet and broil until the mixture melts and the bread is bubbly and brown. Serve immediately.

Note: Use firm white bread—Pepperidge Farm or Arnold, or a home-baked loaf. If you have an unsliced loaf, slice the pieces about ⅓-inch thick.

Serves 6

Adapted from "Bread: The Most Important of All Foods"
Spaulding's Blue Ribbon Bread, 1925

Gary Cooper's Mother's Buttermilk Griddle Cakes

Many of Gary Cooper's films (from *Sergeant York* to *High Noon*) are American classics. Griddle cakes are classic, too (pancakes cooked on a griddle = griddle cakes), and they have an ancient pedigree. Making a batter of grain and water and pouring it onto a hot rock to bake—in the sun, or near a fire—must have been one of the earliest cooking endeavors.

The first American griddle cakes were made with cornmeal. Gary Cooper's mother's griddle cakes are in that honorable tradition. It's hard to find out much about her but if this is what she made for breakfast, she was a woman of merit.

2 cups flour	½ teaspoon salt
2 tablespoons cornmeal	2 cups buttermilk
2 tablespoons sugar	½ cup milk or cream
1 teaspoon baking soda	2 eggs, beaten
2 teaspoons baking powder	2 tablespoons unsalted butter, melted

1. Set a griddle over medium heat.
2. Mix the dry ingredients in a bowl. Separately, mix the remaining ingredients. Add the liquid mixture to the dry mixture. Stir lightly with a fork—the batter should be lumpy.
3. When the griddle is hot enough—a drop of cold water will skitter across the surface and rapidly evaporate—lightly butter it if necessary and make the first pancake (the first batch is the pan's, so make only one.) Cook until bubbles cover the uncooked top surface, then flip and continue to cook for about two minutes longer. After the first pancake is done, ladle out as many as will easily fit on your griddle—usually four at a time poured from a quarter-cup measure.

Yield: 24 pancakes; serves 4 to 6

Adapted from "Favorite Recipes of the Movie Stars," 1931

Banana Waffles

Until relatively recently on the kitchen time line, bananas were fairly exotic imports. They've been around—in the global sense—for over a thousand years, but they didn't arrive in America until about 1804—and that was just one small boat load, a schooner, actually, from Cuba. A quarter of

AFTER ALL, Bread and milk give us all the types of material needed by the human body in less expensive form than most other foods. Therefore the more we can plan to extend expensive foods by the addition of bread and milk, the better.

"Good Things to Eat," Fleischmann's Yeast, 1912

a century later, another boat arrived with more bananas on board. That's how long it took. And about twenty-five years after *that,* the Boston Fruit Company wrapped individual bananas in foil and sold them at ten cents each—a high price, but they were an exotic fruit—at the 1876 Philadelphia Centennial Exposition. It wasn't until 1899 that Boston Fruit merged with United Fruit and began shipping bananas regularly to American markets. Even so, by mid-century, bananas were still exotic enough so that Chiquita Banana had to tell us never to put bananas in the re-frig-er-a-tor. ("I'm Chiquita Banana and I've come to say/Bananas must be eaten in a certain way....")

Waffles, on the other hand, came to America with the Pilgrims. They spent time in Holland before they sailed for America in 1620; the word waffle comes from the Dutch *wafel.* Thomas Jefferson, who brought recipes for ice cream and macaroni back from France, among other things, also tucked a long-handled waffle iron into his baggage. We have electric waffle irons now; the only problem is remembering which shelf we stored them on—or under. Dust it off and try these. They're exotic. And good.

1 cup flour	½ cup milk or cream
2 teaspoons baking powder	2 tablespoons butter, melted
¼ teaspoon salt	1 cup mashed bananas
3 eggs, separated	(about 2 large bananas)

1. Heat the waffle iron.
2. Mix the dry ingredients in a bowl. Add the egg yolks and milk and beat thoroughly. Stir in the melted butter and mashed bananas.
3. In a separate bowl with clean beaters, beat the egg whites until they are stiff but not dry; fold into the batter.
4. Bake in the hot iron according to the manufacturer's directions.

Yield: 12 4-inch square waffles

Adapted from "Bananas in the Modern Manner"
Banana Growers Association, 1930

Butterscotch Curls

Butterscotch is a wonderful flavor: butter and brown sugar combined to make something greater than the sum of its parts. It's something like mixing two primary colors and creating Crayola heaven.

These Curls—biscuit dough curled around butter and brown sugar—are simple and fast to make. They have the old-fashioned innocence that is the hallmark of so many of the pamphlet recipes. And they're lovely at breakfast.

butter for the muffin tins

2 cups flour

4 teaspoons baking powder

½ teaspoon salt

4 tablespoons unsalted butter plus 2 to 3 tablespoons, at room temperature, for the filling

⅔ cup milk

⅓ to ½ cup brown sugar

1. Preheat the oven to 375 degrees. Lightly butter muffin tins.
2. In a food processor, mix the flour, baking powder, and salt. Pulse in the 4 tablespoons of butter until the mixture is the consistency of cornmeal. (Or, in a bowl, cut in the butter with two knives or a pastry cutter.) Add the milk and mix for a few seconds longer. The mixture will be very crumbly. It should hold together when it's pressed; if it doesn't, add an additional tablespoon of milk. Turn the dough out onto a lightly floured surface.
3. Push the dough together and knead it slightly. Roll out to a thickness of ¼ inch.
4. Spread the remaining butter over the dough. Sprinkle with the brown sugar.
5. Roll the dough up like a jelly roll. Cut across into 1-inch slices.
6. Place the slices in the muffin tins—either standing up or flat across the bottom. Bake for 30 minutes. These are best warm.

Yield: two dozen slices

Adapted from "Royal Cook Book"
Standard Brands Incorporated, 1930

Edward R. Murrow's Oatmeal Scones

During World War II, Edward R. Murrow was the quintessential foreign correspondent. He was the voice of London, broadcasting while bombs fell, bringing the immediacy of the war into millions of American homes. As Chief of CBS European Correspondents, his calm and convincing voice had special resonance. "This is London," was his tag line, and it was heard over the radio on Sunday afternoons all across America. He made the transition from radio news to television, and during the McCarthy years, he became a beacon of moral journalism.

These are his Oatmeal Scones, from "The Cook Book of the Stars," a pamphlet published by radio station WFBL during World War II.

²/₃ cup milk

1 cup cooked oatmeal

½ teaspoon salt

2 tablespoons melted unsalted
butter

1½ cups flour (use more if dough is
too sticky)

4 teaspoons baking powder

2 tablespoons honey

1. Preheat the oven to 375 degrees.
2. Mix the milk into the cooked oatmeal, and add the salt and melted butter.
3. Add the flour and baking powder. Mix well, and add the honey. If the dough seems very sticky at this point, add more flour.
4. On a well-floured board, roll the dough into a circle ½-inch thick. Cut into wedges with a floured knife, or use a biscuit cutter or an upside-down glass to cut into circles.
5. Bake for 20 to 30 minutes, or until browned.

Note: If you have any scones left over, they reheat very nicely. They also make a surprisingly good base for blueberry shortcake: gently heat a cup or so of blueberries with a quarter-cup of sugar and a tiny bit of water. Layer the shortcakes: bottom half of a scone, warm blueberry sauce, top half, whipped cream, fresh blueberries. Yum.

Yield: 12 2½-inch circle scones

From "The Cook Book of the Stars"
WFBL, Columbia Broadcasting System Network, 1945

French Muffins

Before there was baking powder, bakers often beat their ingredients by hand for at least half an hour to make them light. In the 1850s, self-rising flour—containing baking powder—was developed. Finally, in 1865, an Indiana pharmacist mixed baking soda with cream of tartar, an alkaline and an acid that react to each other when combined with a liquid by forming a gas. In a batter, they make tiny bubbles, helping the batter rise and keeping it light as it bakes. In 1867, James A. Church introduced the term baking soda (the alkaline in baking powder) to replace sodium bicarbonate, or "saleratus," an American coinage based on the Latin *sal*, salt, and *aeratus*, aerated. Double-acting baking powder came next—the bubbles begin when the baking powder and liquid meet, and finish in the oven, when the heat sets the batter around the bubbles. (That's why ovens should be pre-heated, so that the first batch of bubbles aren't lost before the heat makes them expand and captures them.)

Muffins are the next question. We all know they're little cakes—but not as sweet as cupcakes. In England, muffins are tea cakes. In America, English muffins aren't muffins. French muffins, on the other hand, are definitely muffins—and sweet morsels they are.

butter for the muffin tins	3 tablespoons unsalted butter, melted
1½ cups flour	1 egg, beaten
½ teaspoon salt	½ cup honey
2 teaspoons baking powder	1 cup milk

1. Preheat the oven to 375 degrees, and butter the muffin tins.
2. In a mixing bowl, combine the flour, salt, and baking powder. Add the butter, egg, honey, and milk, and stir to make a soft batter.
3. Place 1 tablespoon of batter in each muffin cup. Bake for 20 minutes.

Yield: 12 muffins

From "Making Biscuits"
Royal Baking Powder, 1924

Date and Nut Bread

Date palms grow in the desert—wherever there's water for their feet, as in an oasis, and hot, dry sunshine for their fruit. There were wild dates growing 50,000 years ago. Marco Polo drank date wine in India; the Egyptians, Greeks, and Romans ate dates; Muslims break the fasts of Ramadan by eating dates. The California date industry began in the early years of the twentieth century. Today we can buy dates pitted, stuffed, and even chopped, and in California, I'm told, you can buy date milk shakes. And we bake date and nut bread. When Chock Full O' Nuts was a chain of shops that sold hot dogs and good coffee, one of their most popular offerings was a date-nut bread sandwich with cream cheese. This loaf isn't as dark and dense as that kind of date-nut bread; it's light in color and texture, but it would still be lovely with cream cheese. Or with coffee, for that matter. Try toasting it, too.

butter for the loaf pan	1 teaspoon cinnamon
3 cups flour	¾ cup broken walnuts
3 teaspoons baking powder	1 cup chopped dates
1 teaspoon salt	1½ cup milk
½ cup sugar	1 egg, well beaten

1. Preheat the oven to 350 degrees, and butter a 9x5x3-inch loaf pan.
2. In a mixing bowl, combine the flour, baking powder, salt, sugar, and cinnamon. Stir in the walnuts and dates.
3. Put the milk in a cup or bowl, add the egg and beat lightly. Pour the milk mixture into the flour mixture and beat well.
4. Pour the batter into the loaf pan and let stand for 30 minutes. Bake for one hour, until a toothpick poked into the bread comes out clean. Cool on a rack.

Yield: one loaf

Adapted from "One Hundred Delights,"
Dromedary Products, 1922

Golden Corn Bread

Because the English used the word "corn" to mean any major cereal crop, that's what they called the grain they found in North America in 1608. Gradually, because this new grain was so associated with the Native Americans, English settlers began to refer to it as "Indian corn." They developed their own Indian corn dishes, like corn bread, based on recipes they learned from Native Americans. Boiled and buttered corn (or even better, poached and buttered) didn't reach American tables until about the middle of the 1800s (and didn't enter the language as an accepted term—'corn-on-the-cob'—until about 1876). Today, corn is grown for animal feed, corn meal, corn syrup, corn starch, corn flakes, and canned corn as well as for plain old corn-on-the-cob. Corn has become a major American crop, equal to the *combined* crops of wheat, oats, barley, rice, rye, and sorghum.

I've had trouble finding a corn bread recipe I loved and could live with—one I could make on the spur of the moment, when I might not have buttermilk in the refrigerator, one that is moist and rich instead of dry and crumbly. This one, from a Quaker Corn Meal pamphlet, is what I've been looking for.

1 cup yellow corn meal	1 cup milk
1 cup flour	1 egg
¼ cup sugar	¼ cup melted butter, plus butter for the
½ teaspoon of salt	baking pan
3 teaspoons baking powder	

HOW TO CARE FOR BREAD

Good bread comes wrapped in a moisture-proof and dust-proof wrapper, which protects it from all foreign odors or flavors.

The wrapper should not be removed until the bread is wanted, then open one end of the wrapper, slide out the bread, and return the unused portion of the loaf.

The bread box should be scalded and aired a least once a week, and should be kept in a dry place.

SLICED BREAD

Sliced Bread offers you the added convenience of bread that is already sliced and ready to serve. No waiting—no knives to bother with—no cut fingers— no uneven slices—no crumbs—no waste. Every slice is uniformly perfect.

HOW TO TOAST BREAD

When toasting under a gas flame, light the oven at least five minutes before making the toast. Spread on the bread and toast quickly, as long toasting dries out the bread.

For buttered toast, have the butter creamed or softened so it will spread easily and quickly. Serve as soon as the toast is made.

"How I Use Taystee Bread," Taystee Bread, 1933

1. Preheat the oven to 400 degrees, and butter an 8-inch square baking dish.
2. Mix the corn meal, flour, sugar, salt, and baking powder.
3. Put the milk in a cup or bowl, add the egg, and beat lightly. Add the melted butter and beat again. Pour the milk mixture into the flour mixture and combine, beating for about a minute. Don't overbeat.
4. Pour the batter into the baking pan. Bake for 20 to 25 minutes, until a toothpick poked into the center comes out clean. Cool.

Yield: 8 to 12 pieces

From "Adventures in Corn Meal Cookery!"
Quaker Corn Meal, undated

Orange Bread

In 1865, an Austro-Hungarian stillmaster came to Cincinnati for his sister's wedding. We assume he was happy for her, but he was disturbed by American bread—low quality, he said, because it was made with poor yeast. Charles Fleischmann began to manufacture compressed yeast, which he and his brother then sold door to door by horse and wagon. In 1876, they brought an Austrian baker to the Philadelphia Centennial Exposition; they set up a model Viennese bakery where fairgoers could see, smell, and taste the wonderful things that could be made with good yeast—and they wrapped the yeast cakes in tin foil so they could be shipped anywhere. The horse and wagon were soon history.

Among the wonderful things that can be made with good yeast is this Orange Bread. The pamphlet notes that it's delicious with orange marmalade for afternoon tea. It is also delicious with cream cheese or butter, plain or toasted. It's a lovely golden color, and has a sweet orangey-yeasty smell that is very nice indeed.

1 envelope yeast
¼ cup lukewarm water
2 tablespoons sugar
1 egg, beaten
2 tablespoons melted
   butter

1 teaspoon salt
grated rind of 2 oranges
¾ cup fresh orange juice
3 to 4 cups flour
butter for the mixing
   bowl and baking pan

1. In a mixing bowl, stir together the yeast, water, and 1 tablespoon of the sugar. Let sit for 10 minutes. It should be bubbly and growing.

2. Add the remaining sugar, the egg, butter, salt, orange rind, and orange juice, mixing after each addition. Add 3 cups of flour, mixing well.

3. Turn the batter out onto a floured surface and knead it, continuing to add flour as needed, until the dough is smooth and elastic.

4. Wash and dry the mixing bowl and butter it lightly. Place the dough in the bowl, turn it over, cover the bowl with a clean cloth, and let it sit in a draft-free place until the dough has risen to double its original bulk, about an hour. Poke the dough with your fingertips—the impression of your fingers should remain in the dough.

5. Punch the dough down, shape it into a loaf, and place it in a lightly buttered 9x5x3-inch loaf pan. Cover the pan with the cloth and let it sit until it has doubled in bulk.

6. Bake at 350 for 1 hour, until the bread is golden brown and sounds hollow when rapped with your knuckles. Remove from the pan and let cool on a rack.

Yield: one loaf

Adapted from "Sunkist Recipes"
California Fruit Growers Exchange, 1916

Sunkist Recipes
Oranges-Lemons

Meat is readily digested because it comes in almost complete contact with the digestive juices. It is 97% digestible. . . .

There was a time when some Americans held the opinion that veal was less digestible than beef or lamb. But research has shown that

Main Dishes

veal acts very much the same in the stomach as do beef and lamb. Occasionally, some individual cannot take care of veal properly, but this may also be true of other foods, and in no way affects the digestibility of veal for persons in general.

"Meat Selection and Preparation," Armour Meat, 1934

Baked Round of Beef with Horseradish

*T*his recipe originally called for a whole bottle of ketchup. (And rings of green pepper with a dollop of horseradish in the center of each, topped with a slice of lemon.) I think ketchup could be one of the great secret ingredients no one tells you about. But a whole bottle? No.

Horseradish, by the by, is in the mustard family, but here it's the root we celebrate and not the seeds. It is undoubtedly called horseradish because it's strong as a wild horse. Cooking tames it. After it's mixed with everything else and has spent its proscribed time in the oven, the horseradish flavor becomes a bit elusive. What we have is more on the pony-radish end of the scale. But still delicious.

1 to 2 tablespoons vegetable oil
2 pounds of chuck, cut into 1-inch cubes
1 medium onion, chopped
1 green or red bell pepper, diced
1 clove garlic, minced
1 tablespoon flour
1½ cups canned tomatoes, chunked

¾ cup ketchup
½ cup water
1 tablespoon grated white horseradish
1 lemon, thinly sliced and quartered
    (discard the end slices, which will be
    all white pith)
salt and freshly ground black pepper

TWO WAYS TO STRETCH BUTTER IN TIMES OF WAR

For our men in service—our Allies—ourselves. Make one pound do where you had two before: Soften 2 teaspoons gelatin in ¼ cup milk; dissolve over hot water. Add 1 ¾ cups top milk (or light cream), gradually beating this into one pound of butter (softened to room temperature but not melted) with rotary beater. When completely blended, beat in 2 teaspoons salt; add 10 drops yellow coloring, if desired. Pack into straight-sided rectangular container; chill until firm. Will keep about a week. Half the amount may be made.

"World War II Recipes," Gold Medal Flour, c. 1942

1. Heat 1 tablespoon of oil in a large oven-proof pan or casserole. Add some of the meat. Don't crowd the pan; remove the meat when browned on all sides, and immediately add more. (Crowding steams the meat instead of searing it.) Add more oil if the pan dries out or the meat sticks. Remove the last pieces of meat from the pan when all have been browned.

2. Add the onion and bell pepper to the same pan, adding more oil if necessary. Cook until the onion is soft and translucent; add the garlic and cook a few minutes longer.

3. Add the flour and cook for 3 minutes, stirring up the browned bits.

4. Return the meat to the pan. Add the tomatoes with their juice, ketchup, and water, and stir well. Stir in the horseradish and the quartered lemon slices. Cover.

5. Bake for 2 hours at 325 degrees, until the meat is fork-tender and the sauce thick. If you need to thicken the sauce further, uncover the pot and cook over medium heat for several minutes. Season to taste.

Serves 6

Adapted from "The Heinz Book of Meat Cookery"
H. J. Heinz Company, 1930

Hungarian Gulasch
(As Prepared by the Hungarian Shepherds)

Before we get to the Hungarian Shepherds, let me note that this recipe is from a very old book that a dear friend has lent me. *The Monarch Cook Book* was published by the Malleable Iron Range Company, makers of Monarch Malleable Ranges, of Beaver Dam, Wisconsin. The book opens with 32 pages about the construction of Malleable Ranges.

Among their advantages, Monarch Ranges had "one thing that every woman appreciates—A TOP THAT REQUIRES NO BLACKING." The upper case letters serve to remind us that women once not only had to keep the fire going, with coal or wood, remove the ashes, and guess at the oven temperature, but also had to polish the stove.

The book includes notes on the design of a model kitchen for an average home. "At the left of the chimney should be a closet for the broom, dust pan, shovel, carpet sweeper, scrub pail, etc....Just inside the pantry door are compartments for flour barrels, above which is a broad shelf and over this may be a cupboard with doors, for cereals such as breakfast foods, tapioca, rice, corn meal, rye, graham, etc....If two maids are kept, there should be a second sink in the china closet or butler's pantry where the dining room girl may wash the better china and silver....The refrigerator should be built in, having thick walls insulated against temperature changes, while the compartment for ice is filled through a small door which opens upon the porch."

As to the Gulasch, as prepared by

the Hungarian Shepherds: "Two hours are required for making this famous Hungarian dish....(It) may be reheated the second day and found quite as good as the first." According to the Malleable Iron Range Company, the Shepherds only used $\frac{1}{4}$ teaspoon of paprika in their goulash ("More or less paprika may be added as desired"), and they chopped only one small onion. No way! Ask any Hungarian! Or even any shepherd. The best goulashes have equal weights of onions and meat, and a quarter of a teaspoon of paprika is just the beginning for a Hungarian Shepherd.

1½ pounds onions, chopped
2 tablespoons butter
1 tablespoon sweet paprika
1½ pounds beef chuck steak, cut into 1-inch cubes
1 cup canned tomatoes, chunked
1 teaspoon vinegar
5 potatoes, peeled and cubed
boiling water as needed
salt and freshly ground black pepper to taste

1. In a large saucepan or stewpot, sauté the onions in the butter until they are soft and translucent. Add the paprika and continue to cook, stirring, for about 3 minutes so that the paprika will lose its raw taste.
2. Add the beef, the tomatoes, and vinegar. Then, stir, cover, and simmer over low heat for 45 minutes.
3. Add the potatoes and boiling water to cover and cook, uncovered, for half an hour or until the potatoes are soft. The goulash will be liquidy—that's its nature; if you like, you can mash some of the potatoes to thicken it. Season with salt and pepper.

Serves 6

Adapted from "The Monarch Cook Book"
Malleable Iron Range Co., c. 1880

Mrs. Frank Sinatra's Spaghetti and Meat Balls

"The Cook Book of the Stars," a pamphlet published by WFBL radio in Syracuse, New York in 1945, included recipes from a variety of radio personalities. There was a cake recipe from Dick Jones, the actor who played Henry Aldrich on the long-running radio show; newsman Warren Sweeney's cookies (the ingredients included "2 Curtiss 5¢ Baby Ruth bars"); a Date-Fruit Salad Bowl from Johnnie, the Philip Morris cigarette page boy; and Spaghetti and Meat Balls from Mrs. Frank Sinatra. Frank Sinatra was "The Voice" then; in 1945, no one would have known who "Old Blue Eyes" was.

The brief biographical notes with the recipe say, "His mother came to this country from Genoa and his father from Sicily. As a lad, Frank had always been crazy about music, but his parents failed to share his enthusiasm for making a career of it…. The turning point in Frank Sinatra's career came in January, 1943, when he signed for a series of personal appearances at New York's Paramount Theater. Then and there, he became 'The Voice.' Sinatra's slight build is kept in hard trim by his prowess at boxing, golf, and bowling."

MEAT BALLS:
½ pound ground beef
½ pound ground pork
1 clove garlic, finely chopped
½ cup grated Parmesan cheese

2 eggs
1 cup bread crumbs
1 teaspoon finely chopped parsley
salt and freshly ground black pepper
olive oil for cooking

1. Mix all ingredients except olive oil. Form into balls (the size of the meat balls is your choice; I prefer something a little larger than a golf ball).
2. Brown the meat balls in olive oil. Remove the meat balls, leaving the oil in the pan, and reserve them to add to the sauce.

TOMATO SAUCE:
1 small onion, chopped
1 clove garlic, finely chopped
1 teaspoon minced parsley
1 teaspoon thyme

salt and freshly ground pepper
1 teaspoon sugar
1 large can (1 lb. 12 oz.) Italian-style
  tomatoes, crushed
1 large can (15 oz.) tomato puree

1. In the oil remaining from cooking the meatballs, sauté the onion and garlic until the onion is soft and translucent. Add the parsley, thyme, salt and pepper, and sugar, and stir.
2. Add the tomatoes and tomato puree, and stir. Gently add the meat balls to the sauce. Cook over low heat for one hour, stirring occasionally.

SPAGHETTI: water
1 pound spaghetti   salt

1. Cook the spaghetti, according to package directions. Drain.

To Serve

On a large serving platter, place a generous layer of sauce. Add the well-drained spaghetti. Over that goes a generous sprinkling of Parmesan cheese. Cover with more sauce, meat balls, another layer of cheese and a final layer of sauce. Serve immediately.

Note: Mrs. Sinatra strained her tomatoes before she cooked with them. I don't. I like their texture in a smooth sauce. She also removed the onion and garlic from the oil after sautéing them. I can't bring myself to leave out the onions and garlic—I want their flavor, and discarding them also removes too many of the browned bits left from the meat balls. Obviously, Mrs. Sinatra likes a very smooth sauce. Now you know what she did with her sauce that I didn't, and here's what I do that she didn't: I add a teaspoon of sugar. It offsets the acidity of the tomatoes. (As well as the seeds.)

Serves 6 to 8

Adapted from "The Cook Book of the Stars"
WFBL, Columbia Broadcasting System Network, 1945

Pineapple Meat Loaf

What an odd idea! But the resulting meat loaf has a lovely, elusive flavor—familiar and unidentifiable at the same time. It's simple to make, especially if you mix it in the baking dish and it's easy to jazz up (with strips of bacon across the top, for instance). It's perfectly good as is, too. You can drink the drained pineapple juice, serve it, save it, or use it to baste the meat loaf—plain, or mixed with brown sugar if you like.

½ pound chopped pork
½ pound chopped beef
1 cup well-drained crushed pineapple, canned in its own juice (<u>not</u> sugar syrup)
1 to 3 cups cracker or bread crumbs, or matzo meal
1 egg, beaten
½ teaspoon salt
½ teaspoon freshly ground black pepper

1. Preheat the oven to 350 degrees.
2. In a mixing bowl (or in the loaf pan you'll be using), combine all ingredients. The amount of cracker crumbs will depend on how well the pineapple is drained. The meat loaf mixture should be fairly stiff, not mushy.
3. Pack into a 9x5x3-inch loaf pan, leaving space around the sides. Bake 45 minutes.

Serves 6

From "Hawaiian Pineapples as 100 Good Cooks Serve It"
Association of Hawaiian Pineapple Canners, 1927

George Burns & Gracie Allen's Lamb Terrapin

George Burns and Gracie Allen's radio program was one of the most successful comedies of its time, as was their later television sitcom. They began in vaudeville with Gracie as the stooge and George as the comedian. Somehow, she seemed to be getting all the laughs, so they switched, and thus was a beautiful act begun. George Burns is one of those favored few who have starred in vaudeville, radio, TV, and film. He died in his hundredth year, more popular than ever, still holding his trademark cigar, and still in love with Gracie.

Terrapin is turtle, but one assumes that the Burns and Allen recipe is for lamb prepared à la terrapin. I wouldn't think that they'd have much in common, lamb and turtles—wooly hair and tortoise shell combs, perhaps—but Lamb Terrapin is a lovely way to use leftover lamb.

2 cups cold, cooked lamb, finely diced or briefly pulsed in the food processor
2 tablespoons olive oil
1 tablespoon lemon juice
2 tablespoons butter

2 tablespoons flour
1 teaspoon dry mustard
2 cups chicken stock, broth, or consommé
1 teaspoon Worcestershire sauce

1. Mix the lamb, olive oil, and lemon juice.
2. In a saucepan, melt the butter. Stir in the flour and dry mustard and whisk until well blended. Cook, whisking, for 3 minutes. Then whisk in the broth and the Worcestershire sauce. When the mixture has thickened, add the lamb. Stir and cook for a few minutes over medium heat to heat through.

Note: The pamphlet suggests serving over toast. Rice also does very nicely.

Serves 4

Adapted from "The Cook Book of the Stars"
WFBL, Columbia Broadcasting System Network, 1945

Baked Pork Chops with Apples

Until relatively recently, when Americans ate meat, they usually ate pork. Pork could be preserved; chicken, beef, and fish could not. Pork can be salted or smoked, and when it's not a fresh roast or chop, it can be used as bacon, ham, and sausage, or to flavor other dishes (like greens and other vegetables), and even to make pie crusts. Almost every part of the pig can be eaten, from the ears to the feet, and on the way, tail and intestines.

In rural areas, people once kept a cow for milk and butter but pigs for meat. Families had pork barrels (for storing preserved pork) in their cellars—thus, "pork barrel legislation," laws passed by congress for the benefit of specific constituents. Other pig-related expressions: "living high on the hog," eating the best of the pork, and "bringing home the bacon," earning what you need to feed your family.

½ cup dry bread crumbs
½ teaspoon ground sage
½ teaspoon thyme
salt and freshly ground black pepper
6 pork chops, center cut, about ¾-inch to 1-inch thick
3 Granny Smith apples, peeled, cored, and sliced
1 tablespoon butter

1. Preheat oven to 350 degrees.
2. Mix the bread crumbs with the sage, thyme, and salt and pepper. Place in a shallow bowl. Dredge the pork chops, one by one, in this mixture, turning each until it is completely covered. Place the chops in a baking dish.

3. Cover the chops with apple slices and dot with butter.
4. Bake until tender, about 40 minutes.

Serves 6

From "Tappan Cook Book"
The Tappan Stove Company, undated

Luncheon Pork Chops

uncheon Pork Chops speak of a time when mother cooked a hot mid-day meal every day, father came home from work, the children walked home from school, and the family sat down together to eat—as they did for the morning and evening meals. Were they happier than we are today? Were families less dysfunctional before we had a word for the condition? We'll never know if the good old days were really better, but the pork chops eaten then at lunch can make us happy and functional at dinner.

Pork chops are ready when an instant-reading thermometer registers 160 degrees; or, when you cut into one chop, it shows no pink or just the barest tinge. There are those who say pink pork is not a danger any longer, but it still makes me nervous and I like to feel absolutely safe about my dinner.

1½ cups bread crumbs	2 tablespoons butter, melted
½ cup canned corn	1 egg, beaten
2 tablespoons chopped red bell pepper	¼ teaspoon salt
2 tablespoons chopped onion	freshly ground black pepper to taste
	6 center-cut pork chops

1. Preheat oven to 350 degrees.
2. Mix the bread crumbs with the corn, red pepper, onion, butter, egg, salt and pepper.
3. Place the pork chops in a baking pan. Divide the bread-crumb mixture evenly among the chops, covering each. A bit of water—1 or 2 tablespoons—may be added to the pan to prevent burning.
4. Bake for 40 minutes. If the topping becomes too brown, cover the chops with tin foil.

Note: This amount of topping can be used for four pork chops, or even for two or three—it makes a very generous mound in those cases, and there's nothing wrong with that.

Serves 6

Adapted from "Housewife's Meat Calendar"
National Live Stock and Meat Board, 1929

New York Ham and Beans

"**F**amous Dishes From Every State" was published by Frigidaire in 1936, and it includes a silhouetted map of each of the (then) 48 states, the location of each capitol, the state flower, and a recipe which "to the best of our knowledge" is especially popular in that state. Thus, from South Dakota comes Pheasant Mushroom Delight; from Alabama, Sweet Potato Pudding; and from New York, Baked Ham and Beans. The pamphlet notes that New York Baked Beans are different from "the Boston method which as you know uses molasses." These New York beans use honey. Another difference is that New York Baked Beans include tomatoes and ham; Boston baked beans emphatically do not. Odd that the use of tomatoes is also the main difference between Manhattan Clam Chowder and New England Clam Chowder: One with tomatoes, and the other with cream and salt pork instead. Do New Englanders subconsciously recall the days when tomatoes were considered poisonous? Certainly the timetable for cooking baked beans is a reminder that in Puritan Boston, no one was allowed to cook on the Sabbath. Beans could be baked all day on Saturday; they'd still be warm for breakfast on Sunday and perfectly good for lunch. Housewives sometimes took their uncooked beans to a community oven for all-day baking—reminiscent of Jewish Cholent, pots of beef and beans and vegetables that also need all-day baking (and that were once often taken to community ovens to cook) and is served on the Sabbath, Saturday.

1 pound dried navy beans	6 cups water plus ½ cup hot water
1 thick center slice ham	and additional boiling water
1 medium onion, peeled	1 cup crushed tomatoes
½ cup honey	1 teaspoon salt
1 teaspoon dry mustard	½ teaspoon freshly ground black pepper

1. Rinse the beans, watching for small pebbles. Either soak the beans overnight in water that covers them by 3 inches, or bring the beans and water to the boil, simmer for 2 minutes, remove from the heat, and let stand for one hour. Drain.
2. Add 6 cups water to the beans; bring to a boil, reduce the heat, and simmer for one hour, or until the beans are no longer hard and their skins wrinkle when you dip up a spoonful and blow on them. Drain.
3. Preheat the oven to 325 degrees.
4. Remove as much fat as you can from the ham slice and place the fat in the bottom of a bean pot or Dutch oven. (The pamphlet's recipe calls for a quarter-cup of ham fat.) Add a layer of beans, and place the onion on top of that layer. Cover with the remaining beans. Cut the ham slice in large pieces and bury the pieces in the beans.
5. Mix the honey and mustard with the hot water and pour over the beans. Finally, pour the tomatoes over all. Mix gently. Bake for 4 to 5 hours, checking at intervals to see if the beans are drying out, in which case, add boiling water. The time needed for baking varies. The beans should be soft and tender; cooking them for an additional hour won't hurt them; under-cooking is much worse.
6. Stir in the salt and pepper. Taste carefully, and adjust the seasoning; you may also need more honey or a teaspoonful of sugar.

Serves 6 to 8

Adapted from "Famous Dishes From Every State"
Frigidaire Corporation, 1936

Ham is one of the best heat and energy producing foods.—Says Royal S. Copeland, Former Commissioner of Health of New York City, now U.S. Senator from New York.

"60 Ways to Serve Ham,"
Armour, undated

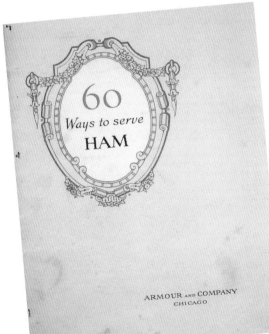

60
Ways to serve
HAM

ARMOUR and COMPANY
CHICAGO

Chicken Patties

When this recipe was published in 1933, it was called Bunny Sausage, because it was made with rabbit meat. Seems a bit much, if you ask me, to be on nickname terms with your meal. Probably because of our national fondness for Bugs Bunny, Peter Cottontail, and the Easter Bunny, Americans tend to keep rabbit off the dinner table. Chicken is another story. Anthropomorphized chickens are not as cute as bunnies. Chicken Little was disaster-prone, and how many other famous chickens can you think of?

Whatever you call them, these patties are good.

1 pound boneless chicken, ground (ask the butcher to do this for you, or pulse briefly in a food processor)

1 small onion, minced

½ teaspoon salt

½ teaspoon freshly ground black pepper

⅛ teaspoon paprika

½ teaspoon ground sage

½ teaspoon thyme

2 tablespoons chopped parsley

¼ cup bread crumbs, cracker crumbs, or matzo meal

1 egg, lightly beaten

butter for frying

1. Combine all ingredients except the butter. Form into 8 patties.
2. Sauté in butter until browned on both sides.

Serves 4

Adapted from "Kerr Home Canning Book"
Chicago World's Fair Edition, 1933

Roast Sage Chicken with Spinach Dressing

*I*t is difficult to admit this, but there's no sage in the recipe for Sage Chicken as it is published in "Famous Dishes From Every State," a pamphlet issued by the Frigidaire Corporation in 1936. Sage Chicken represents Nevada, so one assumes it's named after the sagebrush that grows wild in the Southwest. On the other hand, it could mean that this is a very wise chicken. And a very surprising one, too, stuffed as it is with spinach. Even so, I think it would be reasonable to add a bit of sage—fresh or dried—to the dressing or to the basting sauce in honor of the state of Nevada.

2 tablespoons chopped onion
6 tablespoons butter
1½ cups chopped, cooked, drained spinach
½ teaspoon salt
¼ teaspoon freshly ground black pepper
2 cups bread crumbs

1 roasting chicken

BASTING SAUCE:
½ cup hot water
½ cup melted butter
1 tablespoon Worcestershire sauce
salt and freshly ground black pepper

1. Sauté the onion in 3 tablespoons of the butter until the onion is soft and translucent.
2. Add spinach, salt, and pepper. Cook until the spinach liquid has evaporated. Push the spinach to the side of the pan and add 3 tablespoons butter. When melted, stir in bread crumbs. When the crumbs have absorbed the butter, mix with the spinach. Taste to adjust seasoning.
3. Preheat the oven to 325 degrees. Use the hot spinach mixture to stuff the chicken; sew up or skewer the opening.
4. Roast the chicken for about an hour, until juices run golden and clear when the chicken is pierced with the tip of a knife between the thigh and the body. Baste occasionally with the sauce made of the water, butter, Worcestershire sauce, and salt and pepper.

Serves 4 to 6

Adapted from "Famous Dishes From Every State"
Frigidaire Corporation, 1936

Baked Spring Chicken

"The Sunday American Cook Book" was the first of a series of pamphlets (later subjects included etiquette, home medicine, jokes, and "physical culture") distributed with a Boston newspaper over several Sundays in 1911. Its recipes, by Mme. Luisa Tetrazzini, were "compiled by the Distinguished Grand Opera Diva from her Own Private Collection of Recipes which she has gathered from famous Cooks in all parts of the World." Wrote Mme. Tetrazzini about her collection, "The artistes of the grand opera, like the birds, fly about to all parts of the earth with the changing of the seasons. We are cosmopolitans, 'citizens of the world,' living from time to time in all the great capitals of modern nations. It is quite natural that we should learn to absorb the excellences of life and customs the world over. And so it is that I have come to have my own standards of what is best in the matter of cuisine…"

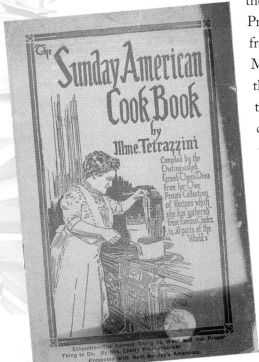

The floured and seasoned chicken in her recipe is baked in the oven rather than fried, and it emerges crisp and juicy—more tempting than fried chicken, the recipe says, and I add, without the splatter and fat. Of course, what's substituted for all that fat is cream. As it cooks, the cream reduces, and after you've poured off the yellow fat, you're left with rich curds of flavorful cream. Ah! Once upon a time, cream was supposed to be good for you. Try using evaporated skim milk instead of cream; just bake the chicken without any cream or milk; or you can also remove the skin—the flour seals in the juices. But if you want to taste this chicken as it was once (on a beautiful April day or in the spring of its youth), try it with a cup of cream.

THE AVERAGE OF HUMAN LIFE

The average of human life is about 33 years. One quarter die before the age of six years, one-half before reaching 17. To every 1,000 persons only one reaches 100 years of life. To every 100 only six reach the age of sixty-five and not more than one in 500 lives to 80 years of age. The married are longer lived than the single. Tall men live longer than short ones. Women have more chances of life in their favor before 50 years of age than men have, but fewer afterward. Those born in the spring are generally more robust than the others. The longest lives are found in temperate climates among country people.

"Guide to Health," Household Instructor
and Family Prize Cook Book, 1898

1 tablespoon butter for the baking pan
½ cup flour
1 teaspoon thyme
salt and freshly ground black pepper to
 taste

1 chicken, cut into pieces, quarters or
 eighths, as you prefer
1 cup heavy cream

1. Preheat the oven to 350 degrees and butter a baking pan.
2. Put the flour and seasonings in a plastic bag. Shake a few pieces of chicken at a time in the bag—if you're using quarters, do one at a time—and mix well, until the chicken is well coated with the flour mixture.
3 Place the chicken pieces in the prepared pan and bake for 15 minutes.
4. Pour the cream into the pan. Continue baking for 30 minutes, or until the chicken is done.
5. Remove the chicken to a serving platter. Pour off the fat, and scrape up the curds and bits of skin. Add them to the platter, or serve them over rice or mashed potatoes.

Serves 4

Adapted from "The Sunday American Cook Book"
The Boston Sunday American, 1911

Turkey and Peas en Casserole

T he subject is leftover turkey. The world's best recipe for leftover turkey, outside of a sandwich, is also the simplest: Mix 3 cups diced turkey with crumbled stuffing (as much as you have, but optimally an equal amount). Mix 2 eggs with 1 cup milk and pour over the turkey in a baking dish. Beat 3 tablespoons soft butter into 2 cups mashed sweet potatoes and add salt, pepper, and nutmeg. Spread this over the turkey, dot with butter, and bake at 375 degrees for 35 to 45 minutes. Serves 6. That's James Beard via Helen McCully. That's for the first night after Thanksgiving. This dish, for the second night, is from a Heinz pamphlet.

There really were 57 varieties of Heinz products once—that was an advertising slogan—and the pamphlet includes a list. First on the list: baked beans. Last: rice flakes. In between: fig pudding, evaporated horseradish, and cooked sauerkraut with pork. And cream of tomato soup, tomato ketchup, and chili sauce. Some things last forever, and some things don't. Leftover turkey doesn't, though sometimes it may not seem that way.

2 tablespoons butter, plus additional butter for the baking dish and for dotting the top of the turkey

2 tablespoons flour

1 cup turkey broth (chicken broth is an acceptable substitute)

¼ cup ketchup

salt and freshly ground black pepper

2 cups cooked turkey (see Note)

1 cup cooked peas

bread crumbs (see Note)

optional: grated Parmesan cheese

1. Preheat the oven to 325 degrees, and lightly butter a baking dish.
2. Melt the butter in a small saucepan; add the flour and cook for 2 or 3 minutes, stirring. Whisk in the broth; then, add the ketchup and salt and pepper, and cook until thickened, whisking often.
3. Place the turkey and peas in alternate layers in the prepared dish and pour the hot sauce over all. Sprinkle with bread crumbs and, if you are using it, the cheese, and dot with the butter.
4. Bake until browned.

Note: Exact quantities don't matter in this dish, and are given only as a guide. The amount of bread crumbs you use depends on the size of your baking dish. You need enough to make a thin crust that covers the top of the turkey and sauce.

Serves 6

Adapted from "The Heinz Book of Meat Cookery"
H. J. Heinz Company, 1930

Baked Fish with Mustard Sauce

enry J. Heinz began selling pickles to groceries around Sharpsburg, Pennsylvania in 1869—very early in the food revolution that accompanied the industrial revolution. Mr. Heinz and his "57 Varieties" were synonymous with pickles and ketchup for years.

This recipe called for Heinz prepared mustard, number 48 on the list of 57 varieties, which listed brown and yellow mustard as one item, in truth bringing the number to 58. The fish is particularly good with whole grain dijonnaise mustard, and that's what I recommend. And that brings the varieties up to 59.

1½ pounds fillet of salmon, haddock, flounder, or sole, cut into six portions
salt and freshly ground black pepper
1 tablespoon butter, plus butter for the baking pan and for the bread-crumb topping

1 tablespoon flour
1 cup boiling water
1 tablespoon lemon juice
1 tablespoon whole-grain dijonnaise mustard
1 slice bread

1. Preheat the oven to 400 degrees, and lightly butter a baking pan.
2. Dust the fish with salt and pepper and arrange it in the prepared pan.

HOSPITALITY IN WAR-TIME

A Hobo Party—For an evening of fun

Serve supper as a "hand-out" from table on porch or lawn or from inside kitchen or amusement room table—covered with checkered tablecloth and lined with leaves or small evergreen clusters. For centerpiece, set up miniature artificial fire with stewing kettle over it (use lighted electric light bulb under piece of crumpled red paper for fire—use twigs for props for tiny kettle). Guests find own camping spots. Supply them with worn tablecloths and napkins well patched in different colors, tin plates and cups—also for each a bandanna for a knapsack for carrying food. After supper all sit around open fire—tell stores and sing old-time songs.

"World War II Recipes,"
Gold Medal Flour, c. 1942

3. Melt 1 tablespoon butter in a saucepan. Whisk in the flour, and cook for 3 minutes, stirring frequently. Add the hot water all at once, whisking vigorously. Add the lemon juice and mustard and cook, stirring, until thickened. Pour the sauce over the fish.

4. Lightly butter the bread and pulse quickly in a food processor to make crumbs. (Without a processor, melt the butter and stir in the bread crumbs.) Sprinkle the crumbs over the fish.

5. Bake for 15 to 20 minutes, until the crumbs are lightly browned.

Serves 6

Adapted from "The Heinz Book of Meat Cookery"
H. J. Heinz Company, 1930

CROQUETTES

Once upon a time, white sauce covered everything. Even breakfast.
It was clean and bland (butter, flour, milk), and it blanketed a bevy of sins,
from overcooked vegetables to yesterday's roast. In this sea of white sauce,
there were stepping stones: they were croquettes. Most often made from
leftovers (in the days before refrigeration), croquettes were ubiquitous. Nearly
every cookbook and pamphlet included at least one recipe for croquettes.
But, like white sauce, croquettes were not all bad. Here's how a World War I
pamphlet instructed thrifty cooks to make them.

*One cup of any kind of tender cooked meat, or fish, chopped very fine. If you wish
the meat to go farther, add an equal amount of
mashed potatoes or rice with beef, mutton, or fish;
soft bread crumbs or rice with chicken or veal. One or
two slices of egg or milk toast that may be left over
will take the place of bread crumbs, or you may use
any cold meat or fish stuffing. Then you need something to hold the meat together, such as very thick
white sauce for light meats and fish, or a brown
gravy for beef and dark meat. The yolks of hard-boiled eggs will make the mixture
richer, and a raw beaten egg will help to unite the materials. Season to taste, using
salt, pepper, lemon juice, parsley, onion juice, mustard, or sweet herbs, but do not
over-do it, for it is nicer when the natural flavor of the meat is not wholly disguised.*

*The mixture should be made quite moist with the thick sauce, because when cold
it will thicken considerably, and after frying become soft again. It should be as soft
as possible and allow you to shape it like small balls, cylinders, cones, diamonds,
or triangles.*

*Then cover all over with fine dried bread crumbs, dip into beaten egg, and roll
in the crumbs again. Fry in smoking hot deep fat, and drain on paper.*

"Left Overs—War Edition,"
Hood's Sarsaparilla, c. 1918

Baltimore Crab Cakes

Very often, at the turn of the last century, if you peeked under your white sauce, what you might find was a croquette—a patty of meat, poultry, vegetables, or fish, mixed with various seasonings, egged and breaded and deep fried. Crab cakes descended from the once-ubiquitous croquette. Only they're better.

There are many people who still flour and egg and bread their crab cakes. I really hate that process—my fingers turn into eggplants, and no quick tip for the process has ever helped me. And besides, as we used to say in elementary school, who needs all that? I'd rather taste the crab than the egg and the flour and the bread crumbs and all the hot fat they've soaked up.

This method is gloppy—well, what's perfect?—but it's good.

1 pound crabmeat	1 tablespoon chopped parsley
$\frac{1}{2}$ teaspoon salt	optional: 1 tablespoon finely chopped
1 teaspoon freshly ground black pepper	red bell pepper
1 teaspoon dry mustard	optional: 1 tablespoon minced or grated
2 teaspoons Worcestershire sauce	onion
1 egg yolk	optional: $\frac{1}{4}$ cup bread crumbs
2 tablespoons mayonnaise	butter for sautéing

1. Pick over the crabmeat and remove any bits of shell or cartilage. Combine the crabmeat with the seasonings, egg yolk, mayonnaise, and parsley. Refrigerate, if possible, for up to 3 hours.
2. Add the red pepper and onion if you're using them. If the mixture seems unbearably loose, add the bread crumbs. Form into round cakes. Refrigerate, if possible, for up to 2 hours.
3. Melt the butter in a frying pan. Add the crab cakes (use a spatula to move them) and sauté them for 2 to 4 minutes, until their bottoms are golden. Turn, and cook for another 3 to 4 minutes. Serve immediately.

Serves 4

Adapted from "Dining Delights"
Colman's Mustard, undated

Fish Curry

From the Hindu word turcarri—sauce—comes the English word curry. Curry powder is a combination of spices; the selection and proportions vary from region to region and from household to household. Some curries contain more hot peppers than others; some include coconut cream or milk; others vinegar and mustard oil—on and on the variations go.

This is a simple, savory curry from an age when a curried dish ranked with the most exotic of meals. (A recipe for fish curry in a Birds Eye pamphlet published 30 years after this one uses a half teaspoon of curry powder.) What to have with fish curry? Choose from: cucumber mixed with yogurt, peanuts, shredded coconut, chutney, sliced bananas, or just plain rice. But there is no one to say you can't have them all.

2 tablespoons butter, plus butter for the baking dish
1 small onion, diced
2 carrots, diced
1 celery stalk, diced
1 apple, peeled, cored, and chunked

1½ tablespoons curry powder
1½ tablespoons flour
1½ cups chicken, fish, or vegetable broth
salt and freshly ground black pepper
1 pound fish (flounder, sole, cod, halibut)

1. Preheat the oven to 350 degrees. Lightly butter a baking dish.
2. Melt the butter in a frying pan and sauté the onion, carrots, celery, and apple until the onion is soft and translucent.
3. Stir in the curry powder and cook for 2 or 3 minutes. Stir in the flour and cook for another 2 or 3 minutes, stirring. Gradually whisk in the broth and cook until the mixture has thickened. Add salt and pepper; taste and adjust the seasoning.
4. Cut the fish into chunks and place in the baking dish. Pour the sauce over. Cover and bake for 15 minutes or until the fish is cooked through. (It will be firm to the touch, and no longer translucent.)

Serves 4

Adapted from "The Sunday American Cook Book"
The Boston Sunday American, 1911

Shrimp Jambalaya

Louisianans are as intense about jambalaya as Texans are about chili or Bostonians about baked beans. Jambalaya is a Cajun-Creole specialty. It usually includes ham; some say the word jambalaya comes from the Spanish *jamon*, or the French *jambon*, both meaning ham, and the Creole word *bal-ayez*, to mix some things together. It's one of those wonderful dishes that can be made with a variety of ingredients, in almost any quantity. It usually includes ham, often chorizo, a Spanish sausage, and always rice. You can make jambalaya with beef, pork, chicken, shrimp, oysters, or crayfish, or a combination; none of those ingredients is more authentic than another. I've used sweet pork sausage here because chorizo can be hard to find; if you can find it, by all means substitute it— sauté it along with the onions—or use both.

1 small onion, chopped	few drops Tabasco sauce
1 clove garlic, minced	salt and freshly ground black pepper
1 tablespoon bacon fat, lard, butter, or vegetable oil	$\frac{1}{2}$ pound shrimp, shelled and deveined
1 green or red bell pepper, cubed	6 small breakfast sausages, browned separately
1 teaspoon thyme	separately
1 tablespoon chili powder	$\frac{1}{2}$ pound ham, chunked
1 cup rice	1 to 2 tablespoons chopped parsley,
1½ cups canned tomatoes	optional, as a garnish
2 cups chicken broth	

1. Sauté the onion and garlic in the bacon fat until soft. Add the red pepper, thyme, and chili powder and cook for an additional few minutes. Stir in the rice until all the grains are coated.
2. Add the tomatoes with their juice, chicken broth, Tabasco and salt and pepper to taste. Cook for 30 minutes. Meanwhile, brown the sausages in a separate pan. About 10 minutes before the jambalaya is done, add the shrimp, ham, and sausages. Taste and adjust the seasonings. Sprinkle with parsley and serve.

Serves 4

Adapted from "Rice—200 Delightful Ways to Serve It"
Southern Rice Industry, 1935

Russian Salmon

Salmon was called the fish of the czars in Russia, but it's the sour cream that makes this recipe Russian—and delicious. It forms a sweet crust over the salmon, keeping it moist. The lemons become soft and edible—a good foil for the fish.

In 1941, Birds Eye offered more than sixty varieties of frozen foods in the little boxes with the bird logo. Among their advantages were peak flavor, year-round availability, convenience, and no waste: When you bought a box of peas, all you got was peas—when you bought a pound of fresh peas, you paid for the pods and *then* you had to shell them. "When the peas reach flavor peak," the pamphlet reads, "our men hurry out into the fields and harvest them. And here is where the miracle comes in. The button is pressed. And, instantaneously, a blast of arctic cold is released! This cold is so intense that it catches the just-picked flavor at its peak and HOLDS IT IN FOR YOU..." On another page, about spinach, "Claims made for Birds Eye Spinach have been accepted by the American Medical Association."

We've come full circle: peas-in-the-pod are what we cherish now. We always paid for the pods anyway, not to mention the box, the wrapping, and the advertising. Even so, who would give up the freezer and its neat boxes of frozen foods? Not me. A delicious vegetable to accompany this dish is frozen spinach: Coat a small baking pan with olive oil, place an unwrapped block of spinach, still frozen, in the pan, and sprinkle more olive oil on the top. Then bake it along with the salmon. Serve with the blessings of the AMA.

FOR EACH SERVING:

Butter or oil for the pan

1 salmon steak, cut thick

salt and freshly ground black pepper

4 thin slices of lemon, seeds picked out

up to ¼ cup of sour cream (half-and-half is fine, but other low-fat is not)

optional garnish: chopped parsley

1. Preheat the oven to 350 degrees, and butter or oil a baking dish. Place the salmon steak in the dish and sprinkle with salt and pepper.
2. Place the four thin lemon slices on the fish, and top with the sour cream, spreading it so that most of the surface is covered.
3. Bake for 30 minutes, or until the fish is firm and the sour cream is lightly browned. (If you prefer fish rare, bake until it has reached the firmness you like.) Sprinkle with parsley.

Serves 1

Adapted from "Birds Eye Cook Book"
Birds Eye, 1941

Think of serving farm-fresh raspberries in November and field-fresh corn in March! Think of eating ocean-fresh fish thousands of miles from the ocean! Or oysters in the middle of July! Or reveling in chicken as tender as the farmers eat! These are no idle fancies.
With Birds Eye they are delicious realities!

"Birds Eye Cook Book,"
Birds Eye, 1941

Preserved Sweet Lemons

*L*emons preserved in salt are a staple of Moroccan cooking, adding the same salty, tangy zest to a variety of dishes as do olives and capers. Lemons preserved in sugar are much more palatable—softer in flavor but just as intense, sweeter of course, and suitable for a wide variety of dishes. If more were necessary to recommend them, more is available: they are beautiful as they wait in their jar, and they make wonderful gifts. It's strange how they manage to be both exotic and super-American—from a Kerr home canning pamphlet published in 1933.

Some ways to use the lemons: diced and added to chicken, lamb, pork, or fish or a vinaigrette; minced and added, with a little of the syrup, to berries or other fruit. You'll find the taste very intense at first, almost shocking, and at the same time a little elusive—and then you'll find many uses for your golden treasure.

2 whole lemons—organic if possible
1½ cups water
1½ cups sugar

1. Wash the lemons well. Place them in a saucepan, cover with water, and bring to a boil. Simmer them until they can be easily pierced by a toothpick. Drain and let cool.
2. Bring the sugar and the water to a boil and cook until the sugar has completely dissolved.

3. Halve the lemons and add them to the syrup; reduce the heat and simmer for 30 minutes. Turn them at least once as they cook.
4. Place in a hot, clean jar. Cool and refrigerate.

Adapted from "Kerr Home Canning Book"
Chicago World's Fair Special Edition, 1933

Three Mayonnaise Sauces

*R*ichard Hellman was the owner of a New York City delicatessen when he came up with a recipe for a mayonnaise that could be bottled. He found his formula in 1903, and nine years later, in 1912, he began marketing his product. Eventually, he sold his name—and his recipe—to Best Foods of California, thus establishing a new continental divide: east of the Rockies, his bottled mayonnaise is called Hellman's, and west of the Rockies, it is Best Foods.

In a 1941 pamphlet published by Best Foods as a newspaper supplement, there are three wonderful recipes for mayonnaise sauces. Each is good in fish salads, as a sauce for shrimp or other shellfish, an accompaniment to poached salmon, a dunk for raw vegetables, a dressing for vegetable salads, or even a spread for sandwiches.

SNAPPY MAYONNAISE
1 cup mayonnaise
½ cup ketchup
1 teaspoon Worcestershire Sauce
1 tablespoon grated horseradish (white)
dash of Tabasco
½ teaspoon salt
2 teaspoons lemon juice

1. Mix all ingredients together.
Yield: 1½ cups

HORSERADISH MAYONNAISE
½ cup mayonnaise
¼ cup grated white horseradish
2 teaspoons chopped parsley

1. Mix all ingredients together.
Yield: ¾ cup

CUCUMBER MAYONNAISE
½ cup mayonnaise
½ cup chopped cucumber
½ cup sour cream

1. Mix all ingredients together.
Yield: 1½ cups

Adapted from "Hellman's Menu Planner"
Best Foods, Inc., 1941

Escalloped Macaroni with Cheese

Macaroni and Cheese is probably a universal comfort food. It's soft and creamy, it's a beautiful buttery color, and it fills your stomach in a very satisfying way.

There are macaroni and cheese theories. Some recipes call for eggs and cream; others are made just with evaporated milk. The white sauce approach is the most universal, and there is much in its favor. This recipe is in that camp. But however it's made, the most important thing about macaroni and cheese is the cheese. Use good, sharp cheddar. Don't—do not—use anything called "cheese food," which is not cheese and barely food.

Processed macaroni and cheese has been around for a long time. Kraft's famous Macaroni and Cheese Dinner was introduced in 1937, when grandma was a baby. On radio's Kraft Music Hall, it was advertised as a meal for four people that could be ready in nine minutes and would cost nineteen cents. A lot of stores sold it for one thin dime. Two-and-a-half cents per person was a hard price to beat.

Some far-sighted women keep a crumb jar, covered with cheesecloth for ventilation, in the kitchen cabinet or icebox. Then they're certain that not one crumb will escape a glorious future in some delicious dish. Just one precaution is necessary. Be sure you use your crumbs.

**"88 Mealtime Surprises,"
Bond Bread, 1931**

1½ tablespoons butter, plus 1 tablespoon for the baking dish and the topping

1½ tablespoons flour

1½ cups undiluted evaporated milk (skim or regular)

1 teaspoon dry mustard

½ teaspoon sweet paprika

3 cups cooked and drained elbow macaroni

½ pound sharp cheddar cheese, grated

2 slices white bread

1. Preheat the oven to 350 degrees, and use a teaspoon of the butter to grease a medium-sized casserole.
2. Melt 1½ tablespoons of the butter in a medium saucepan. Whisk in the flour and cook for 3 minutes. Add the milk gradually, whisking continuously. Cook until thickened, whisking often. Stir in the mustard and paprika. Add 1¼ cups of the cheese, and stir until it melts.
3. Combine the sauce and macaroni. Place in the casserole, sprinkling the remaining cheese in at intervals.
4. Butter the bread and pulse it quickly in a food processor to make crumbs. (Without a processor, melt the butter and stir in 1 cup of bread crumbs.) Spread the buttered crumbs over the top of the macaroni. Bake until browned, about 35 minutes.

Serves 6

Adapted from "Book of Recipes"
Borden's, undated

Hot Creamed Mushroom Sandwich, Tavern Style

Using hollowed-out bread as patty shells may seem old-fashioned to us now—patty shells themselves are old-fashioned—but this lovely "sandwich" was once very modern. In 1928, the Wonder Bread pamphlet noted that we were entering the third phase of the sandwich—first, there was the bread and beef the Earl of Sandwich ate when he couldn't bear to leave the gaming table for the dining table; second came finger sandwiches, crusts trimmed, filled with "the safe and certain ham or chicken or cheese or jelly....But today," we read, "sandwiches have come into their own.... No occasion is too fine, few meals are too important, for the inclusion of the sandwich." There's the Topless Sandwich, "once known only to the lover of Russian food," the Canapé, and advice about choosing good bread.

Made with Bread

The bread you use matters enormously in this recipe. Try a brioche loaf, Challah, or good bakery white bread. You might also experiment with a loaf of sour dough, or seven-grain bread. You can also vary the mushrooms—use your favorites.

1 loaf unsliced bread
4 tablespoons butter, melted (you may need additional butter)
1 pound mushrooms, cleaned and sliced

2 tablespoons flour
2 cups milk
salt and freshly ground black pepper
1/2 teaspoon thyme

1. Preheat the oven to 325 degrees. Cut the loaf into four 2-inch thick slices. Remove the crusts and hollow out the insides, leaving a shell to hold the filling. (You can save the bread you've removed for making bread crumbs.) Brush all the surfaces lightly with melted butter. Bake until the shells are golden brown, watching carefully—once they start to brown, they go quickly.

2. In the remaining butter, sauté the mushrooms until they are very lightly browned and have given up their juice. Sprinkle the flour over the mushrooms and cook, stirring, for

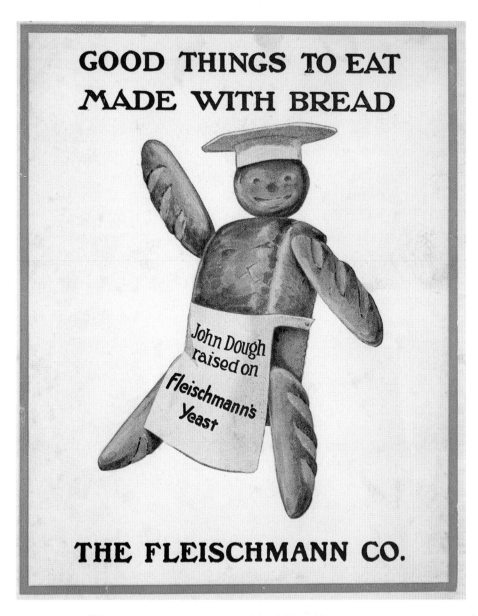

GOOD THINGS TO EAT
MADE WITH BREAD

John Dough
raised on
Fleischmann's
Yeast

THE FLEISCHMANN CO.

3 minutes. (If the mixture seems too dry, add additional butter, a teaspoon or so at a time.) Quickly add the milk and cook, stirring often, over low heat, until thickened. Add the seasonings.

3. Fill the bread shells to over-flowing with the hot creamed mushrooms and serve immediately.

Serves 4

Adapted from "The Wonder Sandwich Book"
Wonder Bread, 1928

Spinach and Noodle Casserole

People have been freezing food as a means of preserving it since before the ice age. But procedures were a little haphazard—and depended on wintry temperatures or a steady supply of ice. In seventeenth century England, Sir Francis Bacon died of pneumonia contracted during his attempts to freeze chickens by stuffing them with snow. Clarence Birdseye, a young scientist from Brooklyn, was the first to develop an orderly and less perilous method for freezing food. On an expedition to Labrador for the United States Fish and Wildlife Service in 1914, he noticed that the fish he caught through a hole in the

THE MIRACLE OF SANDLESS SPINACH!
Every leaf of Birds Eye Spinach is put through a bath that would wash the
stripes off a zebra. Not a grain of sand is left. Why, literally twenty gallons
of cool, clear water are used to wash a single pound of Birds Eye Spinach.

"Birds Eye Cook book," Birds Eye, 1941

ice froze the moment they were exposed to air. When he cooked them weeks later, they still tasted good. He perfected the quick freezing of all sorts of raw and cooked food. He raised the necessary financial backing and the first Birds Eye packages went on sale in 1930. The stores willing to stock his frozen foods were given free freezer cabinets. By the end of the decade, frozen food was a staple across the country.

butter for baking dish
1 10-ounce package frozen chopped
   spinach
$\frac{1}{4}$ cup boiling water
1$\frac{1}{2}$ cups cooked noodles

$\frac{1}{2}$ cup grated cheddar cheese
2 eggs, lightly beaten
1$\frac{1}{2}$ cups milk
1 tablespoon finely minced onion
salt and freshly ground black pepper

1. Preheat the oven to 350 degrees, and lightly butter a medium-sized baking dish.
2. Add the spinach to the boiling water in a saucepan, cover, and cook 5 minutes, or until just tender. Drain well. Combine the spinach, noodles, and cheese, and transfer to the prepared baking dish.
3. Combine the eggs, milk, onion, and salt and pepper. Pour the milk mixture over the spinach and noodles.
4. Bake for 40 minutes, or until a knife poked into the casserole comes out clean.

Serves 4 to 6

Adapted from "Birds Eye Cook Book"
Birds Eye, 1941

To keep vegetables fresh, place them in a deep dish in about two inches of cold water. Take a piece of linen, soak it in water and spread over all, letting the corners dip into the water to keep the cloth moist. Place dish in a window where the air can blow over it.

"Food Economy,"
Knox Gelatin, c. 1895

Vegetables

Baked Carrots and Potatoes

Gail Borden's dream was to find a way to make preservable, portable milk. His first success was with sweetened, condensed milk. (He thought condensation preserved the milk; actually, the heating process destroyed the microorganisms which spoil milk.) In Switzerland, John Meyenberg thought that milk could be evaporated and canned as condensed milk was, but without the sugar. He suggested this idea to his employers, but they weren't interested; eventually, he emigrated to America and established his own company, Helvetia, to rival Borden's. He also helped to found Carnation Milk, which supplied its product in 16-ounce cans to Klondike-bound gold seekers in the gold rush of 1899. Now if those gold diggers and miners had had a few carrots and potatoes and an onion, they could have enjoyed a meal like this one, and stayed to dig another day.

butter for the baking dish, plus	salt and freshly ground black pepper
2 tablespoons butter	½ teaspoon sweet paprika
4 medium baking potatoes, sliced	½ cup evaporated milk
4 medium carrots, sliced	½ cup water
1 medium onion, cubed	

1. Preheat the oven to 350 degrees, and butter an 8x8-inch baking dish. Place the vegetables in the prepared dish, and dot with the remaining butter.
2. Mix the seasonings with the milk and water, and pour over the vegetables.
3. Bake, stirring occasionally, until the vegetables are very tender and the top is lightly browned. This will take at least an hour and perhaps longer. You want the potatoes to absorb much of the milk and flavorings; if you use a deep dish this will take longer, but the result will be slightly richer.

Serves 6

Adapted from "Carnation Cook Book"
Carnation Evaporated Milk, 1935

Escalloped Corn

This is the kind of recipe that is usually introduced by saying it's a lovely way to use up leftover bread. Well, it is. It's also a good reason to make fresh, soft bread crumbs in the food processor. The result is rich and quite satisfying.

This early cooking pamphlet from Lydia Pinkham (manufacturer of little pills for women) is devoted largely to a variety of advertisements. The ads are for the the pills and syrups aimed at soothing the problems to which ladies were once prone. "Don't let periodic ailments drag you down," advises one ad. What's remarkable is not the little pills— once the subject of much humor—but the desperate need for euphemisms, even in a pamphlet designed specifically for women. Periodic ailments are the raging hormones of the last generation, and the PMS of today. At least now we've got the initials right.

Ms. Pinkham helped in the kitchen, too. Her pamphlet included several recipes, and her Escalloped Corn could solve a lot of problems about what to have for dinner.

butter for the baking dish,
plus 2 tablespoons butter
2 cups corn—fresh, canned, or frozen

1 cup bread crumbs
salt and freshly ground black pepper
1 cup milk, whole or skim

1. Preheat the oven to 350 degrees, and lightly butter a small, deep baking dish.
2. Place alternate layers of corn and bread crumbs in the baking dish. Dot each bread crumb layer with butter and season with salt and pepper.
3. Pour the milk over all. (It won't reach the top.)
4. Bake for 30 minutes, until the top is lightly browned.

Serves 6

Adapted from "Favorite Recipes"
Lydia Pinkham, undated

Roasted Onions

O nions have been called the truffles of the poor. Certainly, if they were as hard to find as truffles, they'd be valued even more highly than they are. They're desert island food—if you try to think of the five or ten foods you'd take with you to that proverbial desert island, onions must rank close to the top, along with olives, potatoes, tomatoes, and lemons—Wait! that's five and I've barely begun! I think I'll stay here!

When this recipe was published in 1910, I suspect it was taken for granted that the onions would be peeled before they were cooked—the pamphlet doesn't say. But there's no need to peel them, none at all. They cook very nicely in their skins. Roasting unpeeled onions intensifies their flavor and underlines their sweetness. The following directions are for only one serving, but you can make as many as you like, exactly the same way. You'll probably need more than one—these onions are good.

FOR EACH SERVING:
One large onion, unpeeled   unsweetened butter
butter or oil for the baking dish   salt and freshly ground black pepper

1. Preheat the oven to 375 degrees. Place the onion in a saucepan, cover with water, bring to a boil, and simmer for 5 minutes. Drain.
2. Place the onion in buttered baking dish and bake "until it can be pierced with a straw"—until soft and tender—40 minutes to an hour, depending on the size of the onion.
3. Cut a small slice off the top of the onion—or cut a large cross into it, as if the onion were a baked potato. Place a pat of butter and salt and pepper to taste inside the opening and serve immediately.

Adapted from "Gold Medal Flour Cookbook"
Gold Medal Flour, 1910

Baked Tomatoes

This recipe is an echo of Tomatoes Provençal—beautiful ripe tomatoes, halved, drained slightly, and topped with bread crumbs, olive oil, and garlic. Mme. Luisa Tetrazzini ("the Distinguished Grand Opera Diva") said that she gathered her recipes from around the world, so perhaps these buttery slices are an Americanized version of that French original. This is not to say they are not delicious, for they are, and it may very well be that Baked Tomatoes have travelled the world, like ravioli, wonton, kreplach, and dumplings, wonderful variations on a single theme. The recipe is way ahead of its time—we have only recently taken to roasted vegetables, with their intense flavor and beautiful colors. The difference between baking and roasting tomatoes is largely one of nomenclature, plus bread crumbs and butter, and bless them both.

butter for the baking dish,
    plus 2 tablespoons butter
2 tablespoons olive oil

2 tomatoes, stems removed
½ cup fresh bread crumbs
salt and freshly ground black pepper

1. Preheat the oven to 350 degrees, and lightly butter or oil a baking dish.
2. Slice each tomato into 4 thick slices. Place the slices in the prepared dish. Season lightly with salt and pepper. Dot with half the remaining butter and oil.
3. Cover the tomatoes with bread crumbs and dot with the remaining butter and oil. Bake 20 to 30 minutes, until lightly browned. Serve hot.

Serves 4

Adapted from "The Sunday American Cook Book"
The Boston Sunday American, 1911

Black Beans Havana—Frijoles Negros

The 1939 New York World's Fair was a last celebration of innocence. Hiltler's menance had become clear. The world believed in the promise of industry, technology, and hard work. There were restaurants from around the world at the Fair, from Albania to Venezuela. These black beans are from the Fair's Cuban Village. There was nothing revolutionary about Cuba then, nor is there now about these black beans. They are traditional, for good reason, because they're good, and they're good *for* you, too.

1 pound dried black beans	1 medium onion, cubed
1 bay leaf	2 cloves garlic, minced
4 cups water, plus water for soaking	1 red bell pepper, cubed
1 or 2 slices bacon, a small piece of salt pork, or 2 tablespoons olive oil	salt and freshly ground black pepper

1. See page 57 for directions for washing, soaking, and initial cooking of dried beans. (One pound of canned beans, drained and rinsed, may be substituted, in which case begin with Step 2.) Drain the beans, add the bay leaf and 4 cups water, bring to a boil, and simmer for an hour, or until the beans are tender and, when you blow on them, their skins wrinkle. Drain, saving about 2 cups of the cooking liquid.
2. Render the bacon or salt pork or heat olive oil in a frying pan. (If you are using bacon or salt pork, remove the meat from the pan and reserve to sprinkle over the beans before serving.) Fry the onion and red pepper in the fat until the onion is soft and translucent; add the garlic and cook a minute or two longer.
3. Add the beans to the frying pan with ½ cup of their cooking liquid (if you are using canned beans, add water); simmer for 30 minutes. The mixture should not be dry—add more liquid as needed. Season to taste. Crush some of the beans to thicken the mixture. Serve with rice. (Remove the bay leaf before serving.)

Serves 8

Adapted from "Food at the Fair, A Gastronomic Tour of the World"
New York World's Fair, 1939

Onion Shortcake

*I*f you love onions, this is for you. And if you love onions, it may please you to know that the Great Pyramids of Cheops at Giza are supposed to have been built by 4,000 stonemasons and 100,000 stonepushers who did all that work on a diet which consisted mostly of chick peas, garlic, and onions.

Don't be put off by this recipe's name; this is a *savory* shortcake. It isn't sweet, except for the natural sweetness of the onions, and it is certainly not garnished with whipped cream. It's delicious; it's handsome; and it'll help you build your own personal pyramid.

ONION FILLING:
2 tablespoons butter
2 Spanish onions, quartered and sliced
1 tablespoon chopped parsley
1/2 teaspoon salt
1/4 teaspoon sweet paprika

SHORTBREAD:
1 cup flour
1/2 teaspoon salt
2 teaspoons baking powder
1 1/2 tablespoons butter, plus butter for the baking dish
1 egg, beaten
1/3 cup plus 1/2 cup evaporated milk, undiluted

Uses for leftover coffee: Make Coffee Jelly, Coffee Spanish Cream, or Coffee Ice Cream. Use in spice cake instead of sour milk or in boiled icing instead of the boiling water for a delicious mocha flavor. It may be used in custards, souffles, or in fudge; it may be added to gravy before removing from the stove, resulting in a rich, dark coloring. Use instead of blueing for khaki goods and also for keeping color in ecru curtains.

"Food Economy," Knox Gelatin, c. 1895

1. Melt the butter and cook the onions in a covered frying pan until they are soft and tender, but not browned. Add the parsley, salt, and paprika. Cool.
2. Preheat the oven to 400 degrees, and generously butter a deep 8-inch pie plate.
3. Make the shortbread: If using a food processor, combine the flour, salt, and baking powder, and pulse in the butter until no large pieces remain; by hand, cut the butter into the flour mixture, using two knives or a pastry cutter.
4. Either by hand or in a food processor, stir half the beaten egg into $\frac{1}{3}$ cup evaporated milk. Stir this into the flour mixture, mixing lightly. Spread this batter over the bottom of the pie plate. Cover with the onions. Mix the remaining half of the egg with the remaining milk and pour this over all.
5. Bake for 25 minutes.

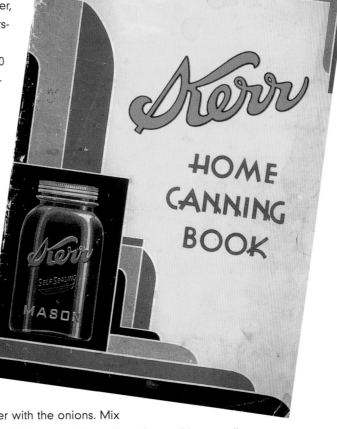

Serves 6

Adapted from "Carnation Cook Book"
Carnation Evaporated Milk, 1935

Rocky Mountain Potatoes

A little potato lore: potatoes came to the old world from the new—from South America to Spain in the sixteenth century. In France potatoes were called *pommes de terre*—apples of the earth; the Dutch called them *aardappel*, or earth apple; similarly, the Germans said *Erdapfel*. This had nothing to do with flavor; it was simply a comparison. There's another story about the names of potatoes: The Spanish soldiers who first saw them growing in South America thought they were a kind of truffle, and called them by the same name, *tartuffo*. In northern Germany, a potato is still a *Kartoffel*; in Russia, *Kartofel*; in Rumania, *cartof*.

Why are these potatoes called Rocky Mountain? I was afraid you'd ask. I don't know. But I do know that they couldn't be simpler, and they are the closest a baked potato will ever get to mashed without taking its jacket off. They're very good.

FOR EACH SERVING:

1 baking potato

1½ teaspoons evaporated milk

1 teaspoon butter

salt

sweet paprika

1. Pierce the well-scrubbed potato with the tip of a knife or the tines of a fork. Bake at 350 degrees until done, about 1 hour. The potato will feel soft when it's squeezed.
2. Cut a wide cross in the potato, and spread the peel back a little. Insert a fork into the opening and mash the potato slightly. Pour in the milk, and poke the butter well into the potato. Sprinkle with a bit of salt and a dash of paprika.

Adapted from "Evaporated Milk Recipes"
Borden's Milk, undated

Potato Hash

Consider hash without the corned beef, or, if you prefer, without the roast beef. That's this recipe. Sort of. There's an extra flourish here: The potatoes are cooked in milk before they're fried. They fry much faster and need less butter, and have a sweeter taste. Save the milk they're cooked in, and add it to soup or chowder instead of cream—it's rich and adds a lovely dimension.

In the pamphlet recipe, a hard-boiled egg was chopped and added to the cooked potatoes. That could be a quick meal for all those nights when there's no corned beef or roast beef in the larder. But more practically, the potatoes without the egg are a very satisfying dish to have when you're in the old-fashioned meat-and-potatoes kind of mood.

It's rarely necessary to peel potatoes. Scrub them well, and cook them virtuously, knowing that most of the vitamins and minerals—and there are lots of them—are clustered right up there under the skin.

4 potatoes, cubed
1 small onion, cubed
milk to cover

2 tablespoons butter
salt and freshly ground black pepper

1. Put the potatoes and onion in a saucepan and barely cover with milk. Bring to a boil, reduce the heat, and simmer until soft, about 15 to 20 minutes. Drain well.
2. Melt the butter in a frying pan. Add the potatoes, and cook over medium heat, stirring occasionally with a spatula—scraping the bottom and turning the potatoes—until brown. Season to taste.

Serves 4

Adapted from "Tappan Cook Book"
Tappan Stove Company, undated

Sauteed Sweet Carrots

Carrots are naturally sweet. A bit of added sweetening makes them irresistible; like underlining a word, or putting it in italics, it's an emphasis. Molasses is the sweetener in this recipe. Molasses is a by-product of the sugar refining process: it's the syrup that's left over after the sugar has been separated from the juice of the cane. There are differences in molasses because there are different stages in the extraction process. The first produces a light syrup with a mild flavor. The second is darker and has a fuller, richer flavor—that's what's used here. The final extraction results in blackstrap molasses, which is darkest and least sweet and, bitter, in fact.

Strangely, the dark, mellow flavor of the molasses almost evaporates in this recipe. What's left is the emphasized sweet taste of the carrots themselves.

1 pound carrots, scraped
1 tablespoon butter
1 tablespoon molasses
salt and freshly ground black pepper

1. Cook the carrots in lightly salted water to cover until they are almost tender—start testing after 5 to 7 minutes. Remember, they'll cook longer, so they should be on the crisp side of crisp-tender. Drain.
2. Melt the butter in a medium frying pan and stir in the molasses. Add the carrots. Cook until they are tender and lightly browned, about 10 minutes. Season to taste and serve immediately.

Serves 6

Adapted from "Molasses Recipes"
Grandma's Molasses, undated

Summer Squash with Tomatoes

Zucchini does just as nicely as yellow summer squash for this recipe. It's a kind of classic—simple flavors, easy to prepare, good to look at, lovely to taste, and very susceptible to variations. The original pamphlet recipe called for the tomatoes to be seeded and juiced. But I like the seeds—they add texture—and the juice adds moisture as well as flavor. It also directed the cook to cover the baking dish, but cooked that way, the vegetables steam and swim in their juices. Roasting them without a cover intensifies the flavors and adds appealing color to the squash. The dish needs to be watched, though—browned vegetables are good; burnt are not.

For this recipe, you need to peel the tomatoes. It's easy: Either drop them into boiling water for 10 seconds, and then cool them quickly with cold water—the skins slip off easily—or scoop out the stem with a sharp paring knife and peel from there.

2 tablespoons butter or olive oil	1 pound summer squash, cubed
1 small onion, chopped	½ teaspoon oregano
2 tomatoes, peeled and cubed	salt and freshly ground black pepper

1. Preheat the oven to 350 degrees, and lightly butter or oil an 8-inch square baking dish.
2. In a medium frying pan, sauté the onion in the remaining butter or oil until it is soft and translucent. Add the tomatoes and the squash. Sprinkle with the oregano, salt, and pepper, and transfer to the baking dish.
3. Bake for 20 to 30 minutes, stirring from time to time, until the vegetables are lightly browned.

Serves 6

Adapted from "Experts Book on Better Cooking"
Pyrex, 1924

Homemade cake is a real food. Bread has long been a synonym of food, and as cake is a refined, sweetened, and flavored bread, there is no question as to the place cake takes in the dietary. Generously represented in most cakes are the food elements from which our meals are chosen— the protein in eggs, milk, and flour, the carbohydrates in the flour and the sugar, and fats in the milk and butter, the minerals in the eggs and the milk.

Desserts

Because of its high nutritive value, cake is most desirable at a meal that lacks hearty food in the form of meat or fat or their equivalents; but as sugar satisfies hunger almost instantly, cake should be eaten at the end of a meal.

"Cake Secrets," Swans Down, 1919

Bittersweet Chocolate Jewel Cake

*T*his appealing cake has much to recommend it: It's simple, homey, and very good, and it's full of chocolate chips.

Cacao beans—from which comes chocolate—were used as currency by sixteenth century Mayans: A rabbit was worth ten beans; a live slave, a hundred; the services of a prostitute, eight. Columbus brought cacao beans to Spain in 1502. Two Spanish queens, Anne, who married Louis XIII, and the Spanish Infanta, Maria Theresa, bride of Louis XIV, brought to Versailles a chocolate drink made from cacao beans and sugar. Solid chocolate bars became popular in England in the middle of the nineteenth century; the Swiss made the first milk chocolate in 1876; and in 1894, Milton Hershey started using chocolate to coat the caramels he manufactured. Six years later, he sold the caramel business and made his first Hershey bar.

1 tablespoon unsalted butter for the baking pan, plus ½ cup butter	1 cup sugar
	½ teaspoon pure vanilla extract
2 cups flour	3 egg whites
½ teaspoon salt	⅔ cup milk
1½ teaspoons baking powder	8 ounces semi-sweet chocolate chips

1. Preheat the oven to 350 degrees, and butter a 9-inch baking pan.
2. Mix the flour with the baking powder and salt.
3. Cream the butter until it is light; gradually beat in the sugar. Beat in the vanilla. Add the egg whites one at a time, beating after each addition until the batter is light.
4. Add the flour mixture by thirds, alternately with the milk, beating each addition until smooth. Stir in the chocolate chips by hand.
5. Pour the batter into the prepared pan and bake for 50 minutes or until a toothpick poked into the cake comes out clean of batter.

Serves 8

Adapted from "Hershey's Recipes"
Hershey's Chocolate, 1940

As soon as the (cocoa) pods begin to ripen, they are removed with pruning knives, very sharp, and attached to the ends of long poles, which are lengthened by joints as often as required. As the twigs are very tough the blow with this instrument must be strong and well aimed, and the laborers must be experienced on account of the particular skill that is required and the fatigue that attends handling heavy poles sometimes thirty feet long, with the face continually upturned.

"Cocoa and Chocolate,"
Baker Chocolate, 1936

Dutch Apple Cake

The edges of this lovely cake are crisp, almost like a biscuit, but under the apples, it's soft and buttery. The cake is very good plain; would it be better with a bit of whipped cream or a scoop of vanilla ice cream? What wouldn't be? By itself, though, it has a sweet simplicity that is very appealing.

1 tablespoon unsalted butter for the baking pan and ½ cup plus 2 tablespoons unsalted butter
2 cups flour
½ teaspoon salt
4 teaspoons baking powder
1 egg, beaten

¾ cup milk
6 peeled, cored, and sliced firm, tart apples, such as Granny Smith
½ cup sugar
½ teaspoon cinnamon
¼ teaspoon grated nutmeg, fresh if possible

1. Preheat the oven to 350 degrees, and butter an 8-inch square baking pan.
2. In a food processor, mix the flour, salt, and baking powder. Pulse in the ½ cup of butter. Add the egg and milk, and pulse again, until the batter is just mixed. (By hand, cut the butter in with a pastry cutter or two knives, and moisten with the egg and milk.)
3. Scrape the batter into the pan, pushing it so that the bottom of the pan is evenly covered, and some of the batter comes up the sides. (The batter is very sticky.)
4. Cover with the apple slices, arranging them in rows or in circles.
5. Mix the sugar with the spices and sprinkle this mixture over the apples. Dot with the remaining 2 tablespoons butter.
6. Bake for 30 minutes, until the apples and cake are lightly browned.

Serves 8

Adapted from "Fruit Cook Book"
Rumford Baking Powder, 1927

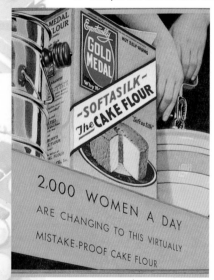